POCKET

MADEIRA

TOP SIGHTS · LOCAL EXPERIENCES

MARC DI DUCA

Contents

Plan Your Trip

Madeira's northeast coast, near Santana (p93)
CAHKT/GETTY IMAGES ©

Welcome to Madeira

Geologically dramatic, bursting with exotic colour and warmed year-round by the Atlantic sun, Portugal's most enchanting island is a place that keeps all its subtropical holiday promises. Pearl of the Atlantic, island of eternal spring...Madeira well deserves its fanciful nicknames and the affection that visitors and locals alike feel for this tiny volcanic island that offers so much.

Câmara de Lobos fishing village (p115)

Top Experiences

Quinta das Cruzes

Madeira's best-preserved mansion house. **p38**

MAURICIO ABREU/GETTY IMAGES ©

Porto Santo

Madeira's sand-hemmed sister island. **p138**

Jardins Botânicos da Madeira

Amazing tropical botanical gardens. **p72**

Monte

Funchal's high-altitude villa quarter. **p84**

Zona Velha

Characterful old quarter. **p68**

STEFAN BERNSMANN/SHUTTERSTOCK ©

LEFT: WJAREK/SHUTTERSTOCK ©; RIGHT: JUREK ADAMSKI/SHUTTERSTOCK ©

Mercado dos Lavradores

Funchal's colourful main market. **p70**

Curral das Freiras

Madeira's most dramatically located village. **p128**

Camacha Wicker Factory
Traditional wicker workshop. **p98**

Sé
Main place of worship. **p40**

Museu de Arte Sacra
Madeira's finest art collection. **p42**

Eating

Eating is one of the joys of visiting Madeira and most will admit the island's fare is tastebud-friendly. Variety was once an issue, but innovative chefs are introducing a touch of imagination in line with mainland trends. Restaurants are of a good standard everywhere; for quick bites, countless owner-run cafes are cheap as chips.

Seafood

Seafood is the big draw, though some restaurants do feature salmon, fruits de mer, prawns and other creatures not from Madeira's waters. Limpets are about the only shellfish native to Madeira.

Espada vs Espetada

The *espada* (scabbard fish) is the eel-like monster that will catch your eye at the Mercado dos Lavradores. Caught at night deep in the Atlantic, this spiky-toothed, jelly-eyed beast tastes better than it looks. You'll only find it on Madeira and some expensive restaurants in Lisbon. *Espetada* is chunks of beef, smothered in garlic-and-laurel-leaf-infused butter, skewered on a laurel wand and grilled over acacia embers. Many confuse the two!

Fancy Fruits

On a trip around the island, you'll see many odd fruits dangling. These are most likely the *anona* (custard apple), the pineapple banana, papaya or the *tomate inglês* (tamarillo). Madeira's own sweet miniature bananas are instantly recognisable.

Sugar & Spice

Bolo de mel (sugar syrup cake) tastes a bit like British Christmas pudding and is eaten around that time. Sugarcane biscuits, eucalyptus-infused sweets and custardy Portuguese creations are also widely consumed.

Best Seafood

Gavião Novo One of Funchal's best restaurants buried deep in the Zona Velha. (p78)

Maré Alta Head to Machico's seafront to enjoy great grilled fish. (p106)

Doca do Cavacas Superb seafood at the end of Praia Formosa. (pictured above; p47)

Best Hip

The Snug Cool eatery in the Armazém do Mercado with weekend DJ nights. (p78)

Boho Bistrô Petite bistro in a busy location in downtown Funchal. (p56)

A Confeitaria Funchal's hippest bakery chain, serving excellent Portuguese pastries and coffee. (p56)

Best Traditional

Regional Flavours Relative newcomer to the scene serving the most authentic of Madeiran food. (p55)

Venda da Donna Maria Food like granny used to make in an imaginative Zona Velha dining space. (p79)

Cantinho da Serra Honestly made traditional food in a rural location near the north-coast village of Santana. (p94)

Best Fine Dining

La Perla Dine on gourmet fare in an elegant *quinta* (mansion) setting in Caniço. (p105)

Il Gallo d'Oro One of Madeira's best dining options with the Michelin star to prove it. (p55)

Madeira on a Plate
Scabbard Fish with Banana

The dish is often served with wild rice or a simple salad.

Fillet of scabbard dish, fried in batter or without.

Passionfruit is an optional extra.

Only sweet Madeiran bananas should be used in this dish.

★ Top Spots for Scabbard Fish with Banana

Gavião Novo (p78) The freshest ingredients and an authentic dining experience at Madeira's top seafood restaurant.

Regional Flavours (p55) Top chefs, perfect service and local ingredients in a superb location.

Casa Madeirense (p57) Long-standing favourite serving purely regional dishes in an ancient stone house.

A Uniquely Madeiran Meal

Gourmets may guffaw at this exotic combination, but no dish on the island is more typically Madeiran than scabbard fish with banana. It's possibly the only plate of food you'll find everywhere on the island where both of the main ingredients are guaranteed to have come from Madeira's sea and soil. Most restaurants across the island offer it.

Black scabbard fish

PIOTR KRZESLAK/SHUTTERSTOCK ©

CERI BREEZE/SHUTTERSTOCK ©

Drinking & Nightlife

Until a few years ago nightlife on Madeira was limited to dinner and a show at the casino, one nightclub and possibly an overdose of sickly poncha. How times have changed, with numerous new bars now spilling out onto the streets and DJs spinning until the early weekend hours, though 99% of the fun is still in Funchal.

Madeiran Tipples

Apart from the island's world-famous wine, Madeira boasts several beverages you might not experience anywhere else. *Poncha* is a local favourite – proper *poncha* should be made fresh and only contain *aguardente de cana* (sugar-cane alcohol – a bit like white rum), sugar, honey and lemon. Despite what some

tour guides might say, Madeirans do not drink it to cure a cold! Versions containing other fruit juices are also available from supermarkets and the wooden mixers are popular, Madeira-specific souvenirs. Swift inebriation can be achieved with neat *aguardente*, but *ginja* – a sweet cherry liquor from Curral das Freiras – drunk from a chocolate cup is a much more pleasant experience. Produced

in Funchal city centre, Corral is the island's favourite beer. Less popular Zarco is the other brand brewed on the island, though many Madeirans drink Sagres and Superbock from the mainland.

Best Drinking Options

Barreirinha Cafe Balmy nights of caipirinhas as the Atlantic breaks onto the rocks below. (p81)

MARK BETON/ALAMY STOCK PHOTO ©

Cafe do Museu Late drinking spot on pretty Praça do Município. (p60)

Mercearia da Poncha One of the best places in the Zona Velha to drink freshly made poncha. (p81)

Madeira Rum House Sample Madeira-made rum in this recent addition to the Zona Velha night scene. (p80)

Best Nightlife Spots

Arsenio's Renowned Funchal nightspot for that favoured combination of

grilled meat, wine and fado music. (p81)

Vespas Cut some shapes at Madeira's grooviest temple to the god of night. (p59)

Casino da Madeira Show, dinner and a quick spin of roulette. (p63)

Cafe do Teatro DJs bring weekend nights to life at the old theatre cafe. (pictured above; p60)

Copacabana Glamorous hang-out where you can fritter away your winnings from the casino next door. (p60)

BRAINSE CABRACH
CABRA BRANCH
TEL. 8691414

Madeira in a Glass
Madeira Wine

Madeira is sipped slowly, often with a chunk of *bolo de mel* (molasses cake).

Madeira wine is served at room temperature in small glasses.

★ Top Wine Experiences

Blandy's (p50) Knowledgeable guides lead tours (with samples) through a winery housed in a former Franciscan monastery.

Pereira D'Oliveira (p50) Check out wine bottles dating back to the early 20th century at this centrally located winery, and try some wine with *bolo de mel*.

Henriques & Henriques (p114) Taste-test wine made from local vineyards and finished in giant barrels.

An Atlantic Tipple

It's what most people anticipate during the flight across the Atlantic's waves – their first sip of the exotic nectar called Madeira wine. Fortified and matured in the enriching heat of the island's aromatic wineries, a well-aged Madeira outguns any mainland port and a visit to one of Madeira's famous wine producers for a free tasting is a highlight of any visit.

Wine barrel at Blandy's (p50)

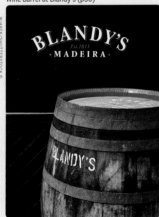

Shopping

Looking past the made-in-China banana fridge magnets and fake Ronaldo football shirts, handmade and homegrown are the watchwords when it comes to take-home items from Madeira. In addition to traditional wicker, wine and embroidery, there's now more artisanal production on the island with everything from jewellery to handmade tiles.

KAROL KOZLOWSKI PREMIUM RM COLLECTION/
ALAMY STOCK PHOTO ©

Mementos Made in Madeira

There's been a real upsurge in pride for real Madeiran-made goods and souvenirs. The bright 'Made in Madeira' sticker can now be seen on many items in shops, but just what does the island produce in the way of souvenirs? The obvious offerings are wine and embroidery, the production of which is strictly regulated by IVBAM (Instituto do Vinho, do Bordado e do Artesanato da Madeira). Cakes and sweets such as *bolo de mel*, *poncha*, jewellery,

Caniçal whale-bone carvings, Camacha wicker and sugar-cane biscuits are other genuine made-in-Madeira items. Now found in every souvenir shop across the island,, cork is not produced on Madeira and is all from mainland Portugal.

Best Shopping

Mercado dos Lavradores Funchal's famous market, bursting with colourful produce from the 'garden of the Atlantic'. (p70)

Livraria Esperança Huge second-hand and new bookstore; Portugal's biggest. (pictured above; p63)

Lillie Ceramics Great, hand-thrown ceramics made

by a sister act from Finland. (p82)

Saudade Madeira Unique items from tens of tiny producers across the island, plus a great cafe and workshops. (p63)

Armazém do Mercado This pop-up space for local producers also holds an organic market. (p82)

Patrício & Gouveia Funchal's classiest souvenir emporium selling the island's best traditional wares. (p82)

Bordal The place to buy traditional Madeiran embroidery and watch this cottage industry in action. (p83)

O Relógio Wicker wonders come in all shapes and sizes at this emporium above the weaving workshop. (p106)

Museums & Galleries

Madeira's excellent museums examine almost every aspect of island life past and present, often in an interactive way. Inexpensive, well-curated and open when you want them to be, these repositories of the island's past are some of the non-outdoor highlights of time spent on Madeira.

ATGIMAGES/SHUTTERSTOCK ©

Quinta das Cruzes See how the other (richer) half lived in the antique Funchal of yesteryear. (p38)

Museu da Baleia In Caniçal, this is possibly the greatest whale-themed museum in the world. (p103)

Museu Etnográfico da Madeira A must for anyone with more than a passing interest in traditional life on the island. (p113)

Museu CR7 Unique Funchal museum (exterior pictured above) dedicated to the most famous Madeiran of all time, footballer Cristiano Ronaldo. (p51)

Casa-Museu Frederico de Freitas This Funchal mansion is a paradise for anyone who's ever collected anything. (p52)

Museu de Arte Sacra Madeira's premier art collection with pieces from across the island. (p42)

Museu Photographia Vicentes Discover Madeira's past through the camera lens. (p53)

Casa da Luz – Museu de Electricidade Whoever thought a museum dedicated to electricity generation could be this interesting? (p76)

Top Tips for Museums ⚠

○ Most Madeiran museums close at least one day a week, normally Sunday or Monday.

○ Surprisingly, Madeira has no tourist card giving discounts on entry, though most museums charge very little to get in anyway, around €3.

○ Some, though definitely not all, of the island's museums have a lunch break, so check the opening times before you set out.

Tours

There's a company selling guided tours on every street corner in Funchal: whale spotting, levada walks, kayaking, diving, city walking tours and much more besides. Keep in mind that with a little planning, levada walks can be easily done without a guide. With other walks, such as the Pico do Arieiro to Pico Ruivo hike, a guide is recommended.

PURPLE MARBLES MADEIRA/ALAMY STOCK PHOTO ©

History & City Tours

History Tellers (Map p48, E4; ☑291 705 060; www.historytellers.pt; 1st fl, La Vie shopping centre, Rua Dr Brito Câmara 9; tour €5; ☺10am-5pm Mon-Fri) Join local English-speaking students for the inside take on some of Funchal's best-known locations.

Madeiran Heritage (Map p48, E4; ☑935 010 779; www.madeiranheritage. pt; La Vie Shopping Centre, Rua Dr Brito Câmara 9; tours €5; ☺9am-10pm) Student volunteers take visitors to some of Funchal's more unusual locations that visitors don't often see.

City Bubble Tours (Map p48, A6; ☑291 782 855; www.citybubbles.pt; Estrada Monumental, Edifício Atlântida; 1hr/4hr/day €26/50/60; ☺10am-8pm) Self-guided tours in electric vehicles are an eco-friendly way of seeing the island.

Tukxi (Map p48, E3; ☑917 229 193; www.tukxi.pt; Rua dos Aranhas 53; tours from €25 per tuk tuk) Tuk-tuk tours of Funchal in the company of clued-up local guides.

Levadas & the Sea

Madeira Explorers (Map p48, A5; ☑291 763 701; www.madeira-levada-walks.com; 1st fl, shop 23, Monumental Lido, Estrada Monumental; half-/full-day €27/37) Professional levada tour company offering a comprehensive range of walks.

Madeira Radical (Map p48, F4; ☑925 871 571; Funchal Marina; kayak trip €35pp) Kayak tours to the Garajau reserve.

Rota dos Cetáceos (Map p48, E4; ☑291 280 600; www.rota-dos-cetaceos.pt; Marinia Shopping, Avenida Arriaga 75, shop 247; adult/child €49.50/34.50; ☺trips 8.45am, 12.30pm & 4pm Jul-Sep, 9am & 1.30pm Oct-Jun) The best marine-animal-spotting tours on Madeira.

Ventura (Map p48, F4; ☑963 691 995; www.venturadomar.com; Funchal Marina) Yacht adventures to other islands in the Madeiran archipelago.

For Kids

Despite Madeira's now slightly outdated image as a destination for old folk, it's actually one of the most enjoyable places in 'Europe' to bring the kids, especially during the northern hemisphere winter. Which kid wouldn't enjoy Madeira's black-sand beaches, countless playgrounds, sunny weather and cafes stacked with tons of sweet stuff?

ALDORADO/SHUTTERSTOCK ©

Loving Locals

It's really the Madeirans themselves who make this such a child-friendly place to holiday – little'uns are more than welcome absolutely everywhere and made a fuss of wherever they go. Bus drivers will rarely take a fare for a child and in restaurants you can be sure of that little bit of extra food should you have a child with you.

Best Museums

Museu da Baleia 3D films, giant suspended whale models and a simulated submarine journey! (pictured above; p103)

Casa da Luz – Museu de Electricidade Electrifying hands-on experiments. (p76)

Centro Ciência Viva Learning by stealth at this interactive centre focusing on Madeira's Unesco-listed laurisilva forests. (p93)

Museu CR7 An absolute must for any football fan. (p51)

Museu do Brinquedo Toys of yesteryear. (p78)

Best Animal Encounters

Aquário da Madeira Go nose to nose with a shark without losing body parts. (p92)

Ribeiro Frio Trout Farm Two things that kids love – flowing water and living creatures – come together here. (p136)

Best Excitement

Grutas e Centro do Vulcanismo Descend into the molten centre of the earth, Jules Verne style. (p91)

Aeroporto da Madeira Plane spotting as you watch pilots perform tricky landing manoeuvres. (p104)

Parque Temático da Madeira Tons of fun rowing boats, clambering around the playground and getting lost in the maze. (p93)

Monte Toboggans Use your air steering wheel as you enjoy a toboggan ride down from Monte. (p85)

Festivals & Events

Live fado music, theatre, international sports events, festivals, culinary events and all kinds of concerts feature in Funchal's packed calendar, with something on almost every day of the year. Though Funchal is the obvious place to head for most entertainment, it's also worth checking out what is going on in smaller communities around Madeira.

AMNAT30/SHUTTERSTOCK ©

Carnaval (Avenidas Sá Carneiro & do Mar; ⏱40 days before Easter) Funchal's Rio-style carnival is one of the best in the world and the biggest party of the year. Certainly the most colourful time to be in the city. Other smaller events take place across the island.

Festa da Flor (⏱late Apr) Funchal's amazing flower festival with costumed processions through the city in bloom (pictured above).

Festa de Nossa Senhora do Monte (Monte; ⏱Aug 15) Madeira's biggest religious festival sees pilgrims flock to Monte.

Festival do Atlântico (⏱10.30pm every Sat in Jun) Incredible fireworks festival held by Funchal's world-beating pyrotechnicians.

Fim do Ano (⏱31 Dec) One of the biggest events of the year, when cruise ships fill the harbour to watch the firework display that uses the topography of the city to create one of the world's most dramatic New Year's Eve shows.

Funchal Marathon (www.madeiramarathon. com; ⏱Jan) Madeira is one of the best places to train for running events over the European winter and now hosts many events of its own, including a full-blown marathon.

Noite do Mercado (⏱23 Dec) Christmas market in and around the Mercado dos Lavradores

Food Festivals Almost every village has a festival dedicated to some local crop or other.

Beaches & Sea Swimming

Some may warn you that there are no beaches on the island, but this is simply not the case. Madeira has natural beaches of volcanic black sand, artificial strands with sand shipped in from Africa and rock pool beaches with concrete sunbathing spots. There are also rock beaches where you can collect pumice and watch the sun set over the Atlantic.

WJAREK/SHUTTERSTOCK ©

Natural Beaches

Praia Formosa (Rua da Praia Formosa; ⏰24hr) West of Funchal and the Hotel Zone, this wild, black-sand beach is the island's largest.

Porto Santo Beach (p139) World-class beach of golden sand extend almost the entire length of the south coast of Madeira's sister island.

Prainha (Map p102, E1; ER214) Tiny Prainha is Madeira's most idyllic beach with black sand and a basic cafe.

Artificial Beaches

Machico Beach (Map p102, F3; Rua do Leiria, Machico) Small, but well-protected beach of golden sand in Machico.

Calheta Beach (Map p112, B3; Rua Dom Manuel I, Calheta) Double arc of imported sand on Calheta seafront.

Rock Pools & Other Beaches

Porto Moniz rock pools (pictured above; Map p90, A1; Rua dos Emigrantes & Rua do Forte de São João Baptista, Porto Moniz; admission €1.50; ⏰9am-5.30pm) Atlantic-fed rock pools in the island's northwest.

Lido (☎291 706 950; Rua do Gorgulho; adult/concessions €5/1.80; ⏰9am-6pm Nov-Apr, to 7pm May-Oct) Funchal's main artificial bathing area in the Hotel Zone.

Villages

ALEXANDER NIKIFOROV/GETTY IMAGES ©

Outside Funchal and Machico, the rest of the island's communities are made up of villages, usually gathered around an old church. Some of the most laid-back experiences can be had exploring the narrow lanes of these places, seeking out cafes and shops, exploring chapels and watching the Madeirans going about their daily business.

Best Villages

Ponta do Sol The island's sunniest spot and a lovely halt on the way between Calheta and Funchal. (p114)

Ribeira Brava At the southern end of the huge valley that tears Madeira into two halves, this wonderful seaside town is a great to explore.

Serra de Água Little-visited valley village on the road between Ribeira Brava and São Vicente. (p136)

Madalena do Mar Tranquil hideout with a beach of volcanic rock. (p115)

Paúl do Mar The pretty, narrow lanes of this surfing village have a character not found anywhere else on the island. (pictured above; p113)

Ribeiro Frio High up in the mountains, this nippy community is the starting point for some dramatic hikes. (p136)

São Vicente This large north-coast village boasts a top Madeira attraction (Grutas e Centro do Vulcanismo), an attractive square, a pretty basalt-and-whitewash church and a rocky beach lined with cafes and restaurants.

Parks & Gardens

A true highlight of any trip to Madeira is visiting one of the island's many gardens, subtropical oases packed with flora (and occasionally fauna) that never fail to amaze with their colour, whatever the season. Only a couple of gardens charge admission.

ROBERT GALVIN-OLIPHANT/SHUTTERSTOCK ©

Perfect Habitat

Gardens often feature a mix of European, South African and South American trees, shrubs and plants, which find Madeira's year-round warmth and plentiful water the ideal habitat to sprout and blossom. In the 19th century, this fact was appreciated by British gardening fanatics who created many of the wonderful patches of green that dot Funchal. Plant-spotting books in English are widely available from Funchal bookshops and you'll certainly need one to identify some of the species that grow here.

Best Parks

Jardim Municipal Lush and verdant tropical park right in the thick of the action in Funchal. (p53)

Jardim de Santa Luzia Undervisited piece of city-centre greenery with a superb kids' playground. (p53)

Parque de Santa Catarina Sloping lawns dotted with picnickers enjoying the views of the cruise port. (pictured above; p53)

Best Gardens

Jardins Botânicos da Madeira King of Madeira's parks and gardens and one of the world's best botanical gardens, set high above Funchal. (p72)

Jardins do Palheiro One of the finest gardens on the island can be found on the outskirts of Funchal. (p75)

Quinta da Boa Vista The best place to see Madeira's famous orchids in full bloom. (p78)

Wine Tasting

Tastings
Provas

BLANDY'S

WJAREK/SHUTTERSTOCK ©

Wine tasting is one of the highlights of a visit to the Island of Eternal Spring. But even after you've sampled the island's sweet nectar, you may find yourself asking the question 'just what is Madeira wine?'. Ideally it's made from grapes grown on the island (otherwise it ain't Madeiran). The basic wine is fortified with a type of grappa.

Tasting Notes

The fortified wine is left to finish in oak barrels stored in a warm place. The longer the wine is kept, the smoother the taste and the higher the price. As it is a so-called oxidised wine, vintners can even take the wine out of the bottles, clean them and pour the wine back in – the quality is unaffected.

Best Wine Tasting

Blandy's (pictured above; Map p48, F4; www.blandys. com; Avenida Arriaga 28; tour €5.50; ⏰ guided tours 10.30am, 2.30pm, 3.30pm & 4.30pm Mon-Fri, 11am Sat) Top wine experience on the island with a guided tour and comprehensive tasting session in the company's atmospheric premises in Funchal city centre.

Borges (www.hmborges. com; Rua 31 de Janeiro 83, Funchal; admission free; ⏰9am-12.30pm & 2-5.30pm Mon-Fri) A low key affair on the edge of the city centre but with a fragrant tasting room and superb, lesser-known wines.

Pereira D'Oliveira (Map p48, F2; ☎291 228 558; Rua dos Ferreiros 107, Funchal; admission free; ⏰9am-6pm Mon-Fri, 9.30-1pm Sat) One of the best places to taste Madeira, normally four types always accompanied by chunks of *bolo de mel*.

Henriques & Henriques (Map p112, E4; www. henriquesehenriques.pt; Avenida da Autonomia 10, Câmara de Lobos; admission free; ⏰9am-1pm & 2.30-5.30pm Mon-Fri) The only tasting opportunity outside Funchal comes at this large operation in Câmara de Lobos.

For Free

A couple of decades ago Madeira was generally perceived as a relatively up-market destination, but oddly enough, it's also a place where your stash of euros will go a very long way. Bus fares and cafe meals are just two of the common costs where prices surprise many. There's also a lot that won't cost you a single euro cent!

ALFRED VELOSA/SHUTTERSTOCK ©

No Cash Required

There are no paid beaches on the island and all facilities at the various places where there is natural or imported sand are free. No churches charge admission, there are no toll booths at the starting points of the levada walks and many of Madeira's gardens and parks won't cost you a thing. Wine tasting is also a complimentary experience, with all the wine houses offering at least two free samples. The best things in life are often free, and that is true when it comes to the island's kicking events calendar. Unless you buy a VIP seat, one of Europe's greatest shows, Funchal's Carnaval, is free for anyone to watch.

Sé You don't need a ticket to get into Madeira's cathedral. (p40)

Zona Velha Wander this atmospheric neighbourhood at no cost. (p68)

Praia Formosa Leave your wallet at home as you enjoy the black volcanic sand at this wild Atlantic beach. (pictured above; p23)

Cabo Girão They may have to actually pay some people to step out onto the glass viewing platform that hangs 580m above the waves. (p113)

Mercado dos Lavradores One of Madeira's top sights is free to visit – assuming you don't buy anything, that is. (p70)

Camacha Wicker Factory It's free to get in, though most people can't resist buying something at this wicker-factory-cum-shop. (p98)

Aeroporto da Madeira Watch the Boeings and Airbuses from Europe swooping into Madeira's airport. (p104)

Jardim Panorâmico Lovely sun-trap gardens in the Hotel Zone with no admission charge. (p47)

Santana's A-frame houses You can wander in and out of Santana's traditional abodes at will. (p93)

Four Perfect Days

Day 1

Start the day at the **Madeira Film Experience** (p50) for an overview of the island's history. Popping into Madeira's cathedral, the **Sé** (p40), along the way, stop next at the **Quinta das Cruzes Museum** (p38), Madeira's best-preserved mansion.

After lunch stroll through the **Zona Velha** (p68), ending up at the station for the cable-car (pictured above). Climb aboard for a glide into the clouds where the leafy neighbourhood of **Monte** (p84) is concealed 500m up. Visit the **Igreja da Nossa Senhora** (p85) then slither back into the city aboard a wicker **toboggan** (p85).

In the evening, amble along the Frente Mar to the black sand of **Praia Formosa** (p23) to watch the sensational Atlantic sunset.

Day 2

Hop aboard bus 31 to reach the astounding **Jardins Botânicos da Madeira** (pictured above; p72). The cafe there is a superb place for lunch with views of Funchal and its bay.

After lunch, head down to Praça do Município, Funchal's prettiest square where you can admire the island's collection of priceless Flemish masters at the **Museu de Arte Sacra** (p42). The quirkier gathering of objets d'art at **Casa-Museu Frederico de Freitas** (p52) is nearby.

For dinner enter the **Zona Velha** (p68). Authentic Madeiran fare from the backstreets of Funchal is served at **Venda da Donna Maria** (p79). For seafood, try **Gavião Novo** (p78). Follow dinner with cocktails at **Barreirinha Cafe** (p81).

Day 3

CICERO CASTRO/GETTY IMAGES ©

Hit the **Mercado dos Lavra-dores** (p70) early to see the fish market in full flow. Having come face to face with the scary scabbard fish, you might need a restorative coffee at nearby **Pau de Canela** (p78), an authentically cheap Funchal cafe.

Next, head for the fishing village of Câmara de Lobos to the west of Funchal. Having watched the local fisherfolk at play, clamber aboard the tourist train to **Cabo Girão** (pictured above; p113), a 580m-high sea cliff with a glass observation deck suspended over the abyss.

Enjoy dinner and a fiery sunset back in Câmara de Lobos. **Vila do Peixe** (p116) specialises in grilled fish, while **Vila da Carne** (p116) is the place to try *espetada* – seasoned grilled beef on a skewer.

Day 4

PAWEL KAZMIERCZAK/SHUTTERSTOCK ©

Time to strike out into the wilds with a hire-car tour. Make an early start to catch the sunrise from the top of **Pico do Arieiro** (p135), Madeira's third-highest mountain. From there it's a short drive to chilly **Ribeiro Frio** (p136) and the **Balcões** (p135) viewpoint.

After lunch at **Restaurante Ribeiro Frio** (p137), descend to the north coast and the town of Santana to check out the local thatched **A-frame houses** (pictured above; p93). São Vicente and the **Grutas e Centro do Vulcanismo** (p91) are a short drive west.

Drive through the the mammoth valley that divides the island in two to the pretty town of Ribeira Brava, where you can enjoy dinner with sea views at **Muralha** (p117).

Need to Know

For detailed information, see Survival Guide (p143)

Currency
Euro (€)

Language
Portuguese, English

Visas
Not required for nationals of most countries.

Money
ATMs widely available. Credit cards accepted at the vast majority of businesses.

Mobile Phones
Local SIM cards can be used in European and Australian phones. EU call rates apply for phones using non-Portuguese SIM cards.

Time
Western European Time Zone (GMT/UTC)

Tipping
Tipping is rarely expected though always appreciated in restaurants.

Daily Budget

Budget: Less than €50

Dorm bed: €15 to €25

Cheap supermarkets and markets for self-caterers

Madeira's buses are an inexpensive way of getting around

Midrange: €50–150

Double room: around €90

Two-course dinner with glass of wine: €25

Full-day hikes/tours: €25 to €35 per person

Top End: More than €150

Luxury double room: from €200

Three-course gourmet dinner: from €80

Private transfers and tours

Useful Websites

Visit Madeira (www.visitmadeira.pt) Official tourist-board website.

Madeira Web (www.madeira-web.com) Tons of info on culture, tourism and events.

A-Z Madeira (www.madeira-a-z.com) General information site in English.

City of Funchal (www.cm-funchal.pt) Funchal municipal website.

Arriving in Madeira

The vast majority of visitors arrive via the following entry points:

✈ Madeira Airport

Madeira Airport is 19km from central Funchal. The journey takes around 25 minutes by car and 40 minutes by bus.

Bus An aerobus by **SAM** (☎291 201 151; www.sam.pt; single/return €5/8, 4am-8pm) runs at least hourly between the airport and Praia Formosa via Funchal city centre and the Hotel Zone.

Car Prerrange rides to and from Madeira airport with **Madeira Airport Transfers** (☎913 756 539; www.madeira-airport-transfers.com; one-way trip €23), bookable online.

⚓ Cruise Terminal

The terminal is within walking distance of the city centre or a short taxi ride.

Getting Around

🚌 Bus

To ride the Horários do Funchal you'll need a Giro card, which you charge with cash at special terminals. Tickets for other destinations are either bought from the driver, or in the case of Rodoeste from the driver or special booths on Funchal seafront and in Ribeira Brava.

🚗 Cable Car

Funchal has two cable-car services – from the Zona Velha to Monte and from Monte to the Jardins Botânicos da Madeira.

⚓ Boat

The boat from Funchal to Porto Santo is the only scheduled ferry service in the archipelago.

✈ Air

The only internal air service in the Madeiran archipelago operates between Madeira and Porto Santo.

Madeira Regions

Mountains of the Interior (p126)
Madeira's peaks rise almost vertically from the Atlantic, with verdant valleys and the levada channels winding through.

North Coast (p88)
In the rugged north, tall cliffs are pounded by a furious Atlantic and huddling villages boast fascinating tourist attractions.

Curral das Freiras

Camacha
Wicker
Factory

See Funchal & Around Enlargement

West Madeira (p110)
Madeira's west is a stretch of ripening bananas, tall cliffs, coastal villages and southfacing vineyards.

East Madeira (p96)
Planes glide low over the beaches of this densely populated area, and nimble-fingered weavers create wicker wonders.

Porto Santo

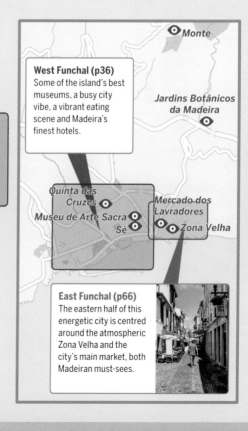

Monte

West Funchal (p36)
Some of the island's best museums, a busy city vibe, a vibrant eating scene and Madeira's finest hotels.

Jardins Botânicos da Madeira

Quinta das Cruzes
Museu de Arte Sacra
Sé

Mercado dos Lavradores
Zona Velha

East Funchal (p66)
The eastern half of this energetic city is centred around the atmospheric Zona Velha and the city's main market, both Madeiran must-sees.

Explore
Madeira

Funchal's Zona Velha (p68) MAGDALENA PALUCHOWSKA/SHUTTERSTOCK ©

Explore
West Funchal

The old lanes, wide 20th-century boulevards and pretty squares of West Funchal are where you'll find some of Madeira's top experiences, its best shopping and most interesting museums. It's also the busiest and most vibrant part of the island with yellow buses, street cafes and shoppers from outside Funchal packing the streets from morning until sundown.

The Short List

○ **Quinta das Cruzes (p38)** *Exploring Funchal's best preserved merchant's villa packed with antiques.*

○ **Museu de Arte Sacra (p42)** *Perusing Madeira's top art collection paid for from the sugar trade.*

○ **Sé (p40)** *Taking in Madeira's top temple, once one of the most important churches in the world.*

○ **Saudade Madeira (p63)** *Enjoying live music, authentic Madeiran food and local handicrafts for sale.*

○ **Casino da Madeira (p63)** *Frittering away your euros or enjoying the dinner show at the island's top nightlife spot.*

Getting There & Around

✈ The vast majority of visitors explore West Funchal on foot.

🚌 Frente Mar and São Martinho are served by buses 01, 02 and 04. All buses from other parts of the island stop on the seafront.

West Funchal Map on p48

Avenida Arriaga in West Funchal IAN DAGNALL/ALAMY STOCK PHOTO ©

Top Experience 📷

Quinta das Cruzes

The Quinta das Cruzes is a quintessential old Madeiran manor house complete with gardens and a private chapel. Originally the home of João Gonçalves Zarco, who 'discovered' Madeira, it was remodelled in the 18th century into a stylish home by the wealthy Lomelinos. The exhibits here examine the life of Madeira's well-to-do from the 15th to the 19th centuries in an aptly aristocratic environment.

◉ MAP P48, E2

http://mqc.gov-madeira.pt

Calçada do Pico 1

adult/child €3/free

🕑 10am-12.30pm & 2-5.30pm Tue-Sun

Garden

Pleasant to explore before or after a tour of the museum, the grounds are a typically exotic example of the type of garden created by the wealthy in the late 19th century. It's a romantically tranquil oasis of mature trees, pebble-patterned pathways, old-fashioned park benches and beds of sub-tropical plants, many of them labelled. Potted orchids grow against the west wall, while on the south side stands a tiny chapel that is normally closed to the public.

Top Floor

The 11 rooms on the building's top floor make up the bulk of the collection. Here, room after room filled with fine furniture, ceramics, tapestry, engravings, oil paintings and jewellery from Europe and beyond give some idea of just how rich the merchant classes of Madeira had become by the 18th and 19th centuries. Highlights include the 19th-century oils of Madeira, the glyptic collection, some from Roman times, a typical Madeiran quinta bedroom and a fascinating section dedicated to Emperor Karl I of Austria, including his priceless Breguet watch.

Lower Floor

Things get a bit chunkier downstairs, with massive wood and hunks of silver replacing the curvaceous Chippendale and gentle fans of the upper floor. Top billing here goes to the Caixa de Açucar, literally 'sugar boxes' – hefty cupboards made from the Brazilian hardwood in which sugar imported to Madeira was packed – a fine example of 16th-century recycling. Other highpoints include items from Portugal's far-flung Asian colonies, a collection of sedan chairs – once the way to get around the roadless island in comfort – and a huge assemblage of Portuguese silverware.

★ Top Tips

o The garden remains open even when the museum closes for lunch.

o There are English-language information sheets in every room.

o All bags must be left in lockers at the ticket office.

o Hidden behind the ticket office is the 'archaeological park', a collection of old ornate bits of buildings that once graced Funchal's streets.

✗ Take a Break

The prettiest cafe around here is the **Casa de Chá** (Calçada do Pico 2-4; ⏲8.30am-5pm Mon-Fri) in the grounds of the Universo de Memórias, opposite the museum.

The **Prince Charles Snack Bar** (Rua Mouraria 52; snacks from €3; ⏲7am-last customer) is a long-established sandwich-and-soup halt opposite the São Pedro Church.

Top Experience 📷

Sé

Madeira's principal place of worship, and one of the city's most popular tourist attractions, sits slap bang in the middle of the city, its tower dominating the skyline as it has since the early 16th century. Though of quite modest proportions, this was once a cathedral that oversaw the largest diocese ever created, one which encompassed all of Portugal's overseas territories.

◉ MAP P48, G3

www.sefunchal.com

Rua do Aljube

admission free

🕐 7am-noon & 4-6.45pm Mon-Fri, 7.30-noon & 4.15-7pm Sat & Sun

Inside the Church

Coming in from the bright sun outside, it takes a couple of minutes for your eyes to get used to the low-light interior of Madeira's top temple. The first thing you should do is look up – the Sé's intricately carved *alfarje* (panelled ceilings) are the most elaborate on the island and are made of Madeiran cedar inlaid with shell, rope and white clay to magnificent effect. The other obvious highlight of the interior is the main altar. Ordered by King Manuel I, it was crafted between 1512 and 1517. Fully renovated in 2014, its 12 Gothic panels depict the Life of the Virgin and the Passion of Christ.

King Manuel's Influence

King Manuel I went to town on the Sé, showering his favourite church with precious gifts. The baptismal font (on the left as you enter), the pulpit and the processional cross (now on display in the Museu de Arte Sacra) were all gifts from the monarch. Very unusual for Madeira is the memorial brass set in the floor of the north aisle. Confirming Madeira's erstwhile trading links with Flanders, where this sort of brass is common, it depicts wealthy 16th-century merchant Pedro de Brito Oliveira Pestana and his wife.

The Exterior

Leaving the dim nave, some parts of the Sé's exterior are worth seeking out. On the south side of the cathedral, look up to find odd barley-twist pinnacles, an architectural feature that belongs to the short-lived Manueline style (1490–1520). The Sé's clock tower has dominated the Funchal skyline for five centuries – sadly it cannot be climbed.

★ Top Tips

o No tourists may visit the church during the Sunday morning service (11am to noon).

o Don't plan your visit for the early afternoon – it's closed!

o Photography is permitted throughout the building.

o Among the cruise-ship tour groups you will spot locals praying here, so show respect when exploring.

o Best times to visit are just before/after a service when all the lights are on and the carved ceilings are illuminated.

✗ Take a Break

One of Funchal's best cafes, Penha D'Águia (p61) is not far from the Sé's tower.

The cafe at Saudade Madeira (p63) has excellent Madeiran dishes made with local ingredients.

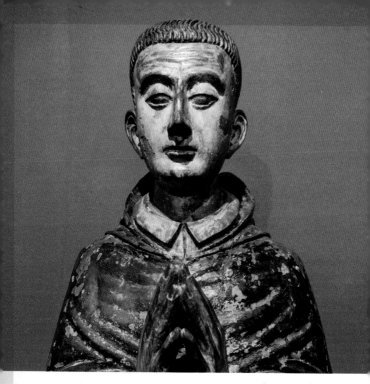

Top Experience 📷
Museu de Arte Sacra

Madeira's top art collection is housed in the former 16th-century bishop's palace, which dominates pretty Praça do Município. Purchased with the proceeds of Madeira's sugar trade, the highlights of the collection are the priceless pieces of Flemish art commissioned by wealthy Madeiran merchants and landowners for their quintas. In the 1950s it was decided to gather all religious art in one place for safekeeping.

◎ MAP P48, G3

📞 291 228 900

Rua do Bispo 21

admission €3

🕐 10am-12.30pm & 2.30-6pm Tue-Sat, 10am-1pm Sun

Holy Silver

The first rooms you enter contain the museum's dimly lit silver collection, thousands of pieces big and small gleaming magically against dark backgrounds. Solid silver crucifixes, monstrances, huge platters and teapots come from across the island but mainly from the Sé, giving an indication of the wealth commanded by the world's largest ever diocese (all of Portugal's overseas territories). The highlight is the late-Gothic silver processional cross from the Sé, a truly magnificent piece of 16th-century craftsmanship commissioned by none other than King Manuel I.

16th Century to Baroque

The museum's middle section is a procession of 16th- and 17th-century religious oils, handless Gothic statuary and baroque sculpture that once graced Madeira's quintas and churches, though a lot of what is on display is from the once very mega-rich Convento de Santa Clara. Look out for the almost life-size sculpture of the last supper, Judas holding a bag of cash, and the remarkably well-preserved 17th-century statue of Isabel Rainha de Portugal.

Flemish Masters

Saving the best till last, the undeniable high point of the collection is the four rooms of Flemish masters on the first floor. Van Cleve's *Ascension of the Virgin*, *Triptych of the Incarnation* and *Triptych of Saint Peter, Saint Paul and Saint Andrew* dominate one room, while Provoost's *Saint Mary Magdalene* from the Church of Madalena do Mar and Morrison's *Nativity* another. Pieter Coeck van Aalst is represented by his impressive *Calvary*, Jesus hoisted high above a lamenting crowd.

★ Top Tips

o No photography or video recordings are permitted in the museum.

o The entrance to the museum is on Praça do Município, possibly Funchal's most attractive piazza.

o Looking from the museum, to the right you'll see Funchal City Hall, which has an exquisite courtyard lined with *azulejos* (hand-painted tiles) and with a tinkling fountain in the middle.

o Adjoining the museum is the small, 17th-century Capela de São Luís de Franca, open Tuesday to Friday from 2.30pm to 6pm.

✕ Take a Break

The Cafe do Museu (p60) in the same building is great for a coffee or a meal.

Leque (Praça do Município 7; snacks €1.80-3.20; 8am-10pm Mon-Fri, to 6pm Sat, 9am-5pm Sun) is a street cafe serving inexpensive lunch fare and drinks on pretty Praça do Município.

Walking Tour

Exploring São Martinho

This downhill walk takes you from one of Funchal's best viewing points through the western suburbs to the mid-Atlantic's swishest hotel via lush tropical gardens, slope-hugging villas and some gobsmacking views, most well off the tourist trail. Around a quarter of Funchalese live in this area, some in grand residences and others in housing projects, such as Nazaré, making this a diverse stroll.

Walk Facts

Start Pico dos Barcelos
Finish Reid's Hotel
Length 4.6km, 2 hours

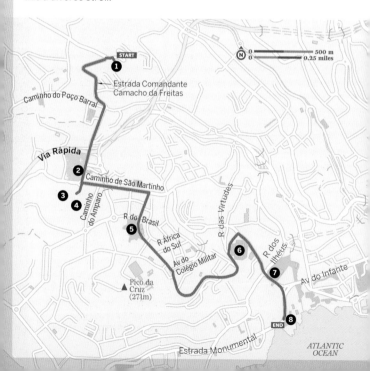

❶ Pico dos Barcelos

Bus 9, 12, 13 or 48 delivers you to the Pico dos Barcelos *miradouro* (viewing point) 355m above sea level. All Funchal lies at your feet and when you've finished ogling the panoramic views, there are plenty of cafes to enjoy, as well as a children's playground.

❷ Cemitério de São Martinho

The **Cemitério de São Martinho** (Caminho de São Martinho; ⏱9am-5pm) is well off the tourist path, making it all the more fascinating to visit. Funchal's wealthy were once laid to rest here, their coffins stacked in family *jazigos* – sepulchres resembling small ornate sheds, some in art nouveau and functionalist styles.

❸ Igreja de São Martinho

High above west Funchal rises the whitewashed spire of the **Igreja de São Martinho** (www.paroquias martinho.com; Rua da Igreja; ⏱3-7pm Mon-Fri, 9am-noon & 4-8pm Sat, 9am-1pm Sun), a big, early-20th-century creation. The interior is highly decorative neoclassical in design and the grounds have great views.

❹ Jardim de São Martinho

Just below the church you'll discover the lovely **Jardim de São Martinho** (Caminha da Igreja Nova; ⏱7am-9pm Apr-Oct, 8am-7pm Nov-Mar), a south-facing, artificially created set of gardens with thousands of exotic plants tumbling down a terraced hillside to a children's playground.

❺ Mata da Nazaré

The Mata da Nazaré is a forgotten piece of Funchal greenery sporting lots of palm trees and generous stretches of grass, a good spot to shake out the picnic blanket. The only attraction here is a monument to Madeirans who died fighting in Portugal's colonies between the 1950s and 1974.

❻ Estádio dos Barreiros

Head down Rua dos Estados Unidos da América to the newly rebuilt Estádio dos Barreiros, home to top-tier soccer outfit Marítimo. Matches normally take place on Sunday afternoons and the atmosphere, whipped up by samba drums and loudhailers, can be pretty good.

❼ Quinta Magnólia Gardens

The erstwhile estate of a British merchant family, the Quinta Magnólia Gardens are pleasant enough, though the whole caboodle, sports facilities and all, was receiving an update when we last visited.

❽ Reid's Hotel

Reid's Hotel, the brainchild of Scotsman William Reid, was Funchal's first hotel. Churchill, Gregory Peck and several crowned heads, among illustrious others, all stayed here and it still attracts a smart set to its formal tea terrace (p59) and sumptuous rooms overlooking Funchal Bay.

Wander along Frente Mar

This sun-drenched walk along the seafront of Funchal's Hotel Zone is the perfect lazy first-day stroll. These south-facing slopes are carpeted in tropical and subtropical flora, with lizards darting between rocks and bees busy making exotic honey. The sheer number of cafes, restaurants, beaches and viewpoints along this route provides ample excuse for never reaching the end.

Walk Facts

Start Lido
Finiah Praia Formosa
Length 3.5km, 2 hours

Pico da
Cruz
(271m)

Estrada Monumental

Estrada Monumental

R. do Gorgulho

END
8

7

R. da Ponta da Cruz

6

5

4

3

2

1
START

ATLANTIC OCEAN

0   500 m
0   0.25 miles

❶ Lido

Reopened in 2016 after a major revamp, the popular Lido has a large pool, kids pools, sunbathing areas and sunbeds for hire, though there's limited access to the sea. Nearby, a large, palm-fringed grassy area is where football games – tourist kids versus locals – sometimes kick off.

❷ Ilhéu do Lido

Just west of the Lido area, the tall tower of rock sticking up offshore is the picturesque Ilhéu do Lido, opposite which is a sunbathing area and stony beach popular with locals and visiting families.

❸ Jardim Panorâmico

Up a set of steps from the seafront, the terraced **Jardim Panorâmico** (Estrada Monumental; admission free; ⊙7am-10pm; ⊞) is a sun-catching spot ideal for a lazy afternoon with a book. It's also a superb halt with children as there are go-karts, a bouncy castle and crazy golf, as well as a couple of cafes nearby.

❹ Clube Naval do Funchal

A huge sweep of purple bougainvillea announces your arrival at the **Clube Naval do Funchal** (www.clubenavaldofunchal.com; Rua da Quinta Calaça 32; per day non-members €10; ⊙9am-7pm), a leisure complex with a restaurant, children's pool, sports facilities, saltwater pool, playground and diving centre.

❺ Complexo Balnear Ponta Gorda

A more down-to-earth swimming area is located at Ponta Gorda – the **Complexo Balnear Ponta Gorda** (Ponta Gorda; adult/child €5/free; ⊙9am-6pm). Popular with locals, the pools, cafe-bar, table-tennis area and concrete 'beach' remain open year-round.

❻ Ponta da Cruz

A statue of João Gonçalves Zarco looks out towards Cabo Girão from Ponta da Cruz, a huge chunk of rock jutting out into the Atlantic. Bus 2 will take you back to the Lido from here; otherwise, carry on down the steps beyond the statue.

❼ Doca do Cavacas

Using only locally caught seafood in its dishes, **Doca do Cavacas** (Rua da Ponta da Cruz; mains €4-16; ⊙10am-midnight Tue-Sun) juts out of the volcanic rock like an ocean-going liner. The semicircular glazed dining room provides 180-degree Atlantic vistas as you munch on its offerings.

❽ Praia Formosa

From the Doca do Cavacas a tunnel bores through the rock to Madeira's biggest beach, Praia Formosa. This starts out as a field of basalt rocks that gives way to a wild stretch of black volcanic sand.

A **B** **C** **D**

1

2

Cç do Pico

13 ◉

Fortaleza ◉ do Pico

Quinta das Cruzes

🛍51
🛍55

3

R das Maravilhas

R Reis Gome

R Dr Brito Câmara

R Calouste Gulbenkien

4

R do Jasmineiro

Av. Luís de Camões

28 ✖

Av do Infante

Parque de **14** Santa Catarina ◉

5

◉19 ✖22
🛍35 ✖27
🛍45 ✖29
🛍53

★47

36 ☕

Muse CR.

City Bubble Tours

17 ◉

44 ☕D Amélia

Estrada Monumental

☕43

R Imperatriz **24** ✖

Av Sá Carneiro

6

R Carvalho Araujo

A **B** **C** **D**

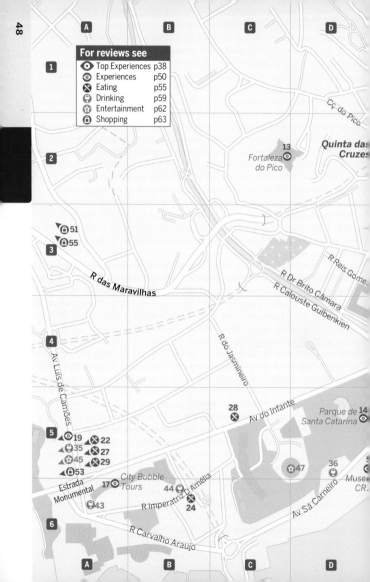

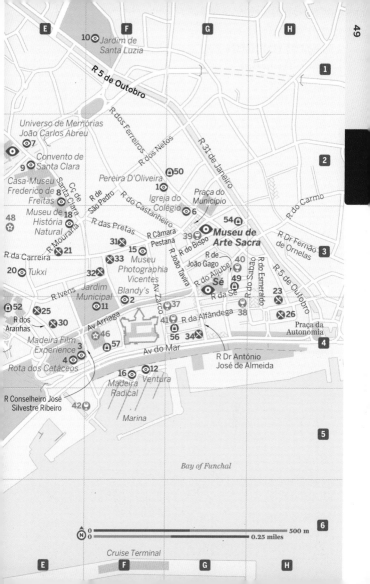

Experiences

Pereira D'Oliveira
WINERY

1 ◉ **MAP P48, F2**

Run by the fifth generation of the D'Oliveira family, this is Funchal's most easily accessible wine experience. Anyone can enter the strongly aromatic barrel room in central Funchal and try almost as much wine as they please, usually accompanied by a wedge of *bolo de mel* (molasses cake) and crackers. Bottles of wine dating back to the early 20th century line the walls and the company offers good shipping deals on wine you buy. (☏291 228 558; Rua dos Ferreiros 107, Funchal; admission free; ⊙9am-6pm Mon-Fri, 9.30-1pm Sat)

Blandy's
WINERY

2 ◉ **MAP P48, F4**

Housed in the Adegas de São Francisco, the former Franciscan monastery, Blandy's brings together the British-Madeiran wine companies that were given special trading rights with Britain in the 17th century. The best known of Madeira's wine experiences, its 45-minute tours are led by clued-up guides and there are two free samples at the end. (www.blandys.com; Avenida Arriaga 28; tour €5.50; ⊙guided tours 10.30am, 2.30pm, 3.30pm & 4.30pm Mon-Fri, 11am Sat)

History Tellers
WALKING

Informative walking tours of Funchal given by clued-up local student voluteers. All proceeds go into scholarships and the student union at the University of Madeira. Book at the Naturalmente Português shop at the La Vie shopping centre (see 52 🔒 Map p48, E4) or in the foyer of the university. (☏291 705 060; www.historytellers.pt; 1st fl, La Vie shopping centre, Rua Dr Brito Câmara 9; tours €5; ⊙10am-5pm Mon-Fri)

Madeiran Heritage
TOURS

This interesting initiative runs tours to several places you wouldn't ordinarily get to see, such as the Quinta Vigia (president's residence), the Madeiran legislative assembly building, City Hall and the Jesuit College. The guides are student volunteers from Madeira Uni. Check the website for meeting points (see 52 🔒 Map p48, E4), tour dates and times. (☏935 010 779; www.madeiranheritage.pt; La Vie Shopping Centre, Rua Dr Brito Câmara 9; tours €5; ⊙9am-10pm)

Madeira Film Experience
CULTURAL CENTRE

3 ◉ **MAP P48, E4**

This undervisited attraction ambitiously promises 'the island's history in 30 minutes' and, it must be said, doesn't disappoint. With a soundtrack in several languages fed to headphones, this superbly produced and animated film takes you through the main periods of the island's past in a dramatic, colourful and informative way, leaving you panting for breath and eager to learn more. (📞291 222 748; www.madeirafilmexperience.com; Marina Shopping, Rua Conselheiro José Silvestre Ribeiro 1, east entrance; admission €5; ⊙10.15am-5pm)

Rota dos Cetáceos WILDLIFE

4 ◉ MAP P48, E4

These four-hour whale- and dolphin-watching tours in the company of marine biologists are for those who are serious about spotting Atlantic wildlife. If you don't see what you came to see, the company will take you again free of charge. (📞291 280 600; www.rota-dos-cetaceos.pt; Marinia Shopping, Avenida Arriaga 75, shop 247; adult/child €49.50/34.50; ⊙trips 8.45am, 12.30pm & 4pm Jul-Sep, 9am & 1.30pm Oct-Jun)

Museu CR7 MUSEUM

5 ◉ MAP P48, D5

If, after a few days in Funchal, the fact has somehow escaped your attention, here you will quickly found out that the world's greatest footballer, Cristiano Ronaldo was born and grew up here in Funchal. This museum is basically a glitzy public store cupboard for all the tens of cups, man-of-the-match awards, winner's medals, fan letters, hat-trick balls, shirts and golden balls he has acquired throughout his illustrious footballing career. (📞291 639 880; www.museucr7.com; Avida Sá Carneiro – Praça do Mar 27; admission €5; ⊙10am-6pm Mon-Sat; 👶)

Pereira D'Oliveira

Ronaldo's Statue

Looking into the entrance of the Museu CR7, you cannot fail to notice the Ronaldo statue, a bronze of Funchal's most illustrious son, unveiled in his presence in December 2014 in a different location. It depicts the soccer star in his famous 'ready for it' pose, but many have commented on how well endowed the figure is, and they're not talking about his talent with a ball. There was a suggestion the statue could be altered to remove the offending area but the powers that be decided against it. Rubbing the statue in certain areas is said to bring good luck.

Igreja do Colégio CHURCH

6 ◎ MAP P48, G3

Funchal's Jesuit Church dominates the city's prettiest square, Praça do Município. No surface is left unadorned in the baroque interior with its azulejos, painted arches and trompe l'oeil ceiling. The tower can be climbed, though there are better vantage points in the city. (Praça do Município; tower €1; ⏱8am-8pm)

Universo de Memórias João Carlos Abreu MUSEUM

7 ◎ MAP P48, E2

Housed in an elegant 19th-century mansion, this museum–arts centre is another repository of knick-knacks donated to the city by an avid collector, this time João Carlos Abreu – journalist, writer, politician, actor, artist, former minister of tourism and, evidently, keen traveller and souvenir acquirer. However, these are no ordinary mementos – room after room is packed with wonderful objects, many works of art. (Calçada do Pico 2; adult/concession €3.50/2; ⏱10am-5pm Mon-Fri)

Casa-Museu Frederico de Freitas MUSEUM

8 ◎ MAP P48, E2

Built by the counts of Calçada in the 17th century, this tasteful mansion was purchased by a local lawyer, Frederico de Freitas, in the 1940s. An avid collector of just about anything, over the next three decades he proceeded to fill its rooms with antiques and knick-knacks from his travels around the world. Wander the high-ceilinged rooms, each one a shrine to de Freitas' good taste, packed with fine furniture, carpets and valuable trinkets. (Calçada de Santa Clara 7; adult/concession €3/1.50; ⏱10am-5.30pm Tue-Sat)

Convento de Santa Clara CONVENT

9 ◎ MAP P48, E2

The highlight of this 15th-century convent, once the island's richest, is one of the island's most attractive churches, with floor to ceiling *azulejos* tiles and waxy hardwood floors. Knock at the adjacent convent door for a short guided tour of the rest of the complex, given by one of the resident nuns. (Calçada de Santa Clara; admission €2; ⏱10am-noon & 3-5pm)

Jardim de Santa Luzia PARK

10 ⊙ MAP P48, F1

Created from an old sugar works – hence the huge chimney in the middle and old bits of machinery scattered around the place – this undervisited city-centre oasis has heaps of exotic plant life, its own levada, a great playground and a cafe. It also hosts an occasional Sunday flea market. (Rua 31 de Janeiro; ⏱8am-midnight)

Jardim Municipal PARK

11 ⊙ MAP P48, F4

Verdant old park in the city centre, created on the site of the Convent of San Francisco, with tens of exotic labelled trees, twittering birds, basalt pebble paths, a cafe, toilet and a stage where many events are held throughout the year, including part of the Carnaval. (Avenida Arriaga; ⏱24hr)

Ventura ADVENTURE

12 ⊙ MAP P48, F4

One of the few companies running yacht tours to the uninhabited Desertas and Selvagens islands, as well as birdwatching trips, dolphin- and whale-spotting tours

and canyoning outings into the mountainous interior. (☎963 691 995; www.venturadomar.com; Funchal Marina)

Fortaleza do Pico FORTRESS

13 ⊙ MAP P48, C2

Easy to spot, but taxing to reach, it's worth the slog up to this rock-top fortress northwest of the city centre for the stupendous views, possibly the best of Funchal in its entirety you'll get anywhere. Built in the 17th century as a surveillance point, the building has been Portuguese navy property for the last seven decades. Undervisited, it now has a cafe and an exhibition but also serves as a tranquil, if sometimes windy, picnic venue. (Rua do Castelo; admission free; ⏱10am-6pm Tue-Sat)

Parque de Santa Catarina PARK

14 ⊙ MAP P48, D5

This large sloping park contains a well-equipped children's playground, a cafe and Madeira's first chapel. It's a lovely picnic spot amid exotic greenery. (Avenida do Infante; ⏱7am-9pm Apr-Sep, to 7pm Oct-Mar; 👶)

Museu Photographia Vicentes MUSEUM

15 ⊙ MAP P48, F3

Set up by Vicente Gomes da Silva in 1865, this exquisitely preserved photographic studio, above a shady cobbled courtyard, was in

PARK DALE/ALAMY STOCK PHOTO

Tukxi tour in Funchal

use until 1982. The exhibitions of yesteryear's photographic equipment are interesting enough, but the real treasures here are the 800,000 images, mostly from the 20th century – by far the most valuable record of island life in existence. The museum was under renovation at the time of research but was set to reopen in 2019. (Rua da Carreira 43)

Madeira Radical KAYAKING

16 MAP P48, F4

This small company runs guided sea kayaking trips for between two and six people mostly to the Garajau reserve in the mornings. Other routes and times are available on request. (📞925 871 571; Funchal Marina; kayak trips per person €35)

City Bubble Tours DRIVING

17 ⊚ MAP P48, A6

These electric, two-seater Renault Twizys have become a popular, fun and eco-friendly way of seeing Madeira. Preset tours are GPS-guided and there are charging points at strategic locations around the island. (📞291 782 855; www.citybubbles.pt; Estrada Monumental, Edifício Atlântida; 1hr/4hr/day €26/50/60; ⏱10am-8pm)

Museu de História Natural MUSEUM

18 ⊚ MAP P48, E3

This old-fashioned museum, housed (in classic Funchal fashion) in a surplus palace, has an ageing aquarium on the ground floor, and stuffed local fauna, including many sea creatures, upstairs. Highlights include an interesting 3D map of Madeira and a display of spiders you definitely didn't know inhabited the island before you booked your holiday. The museum is also a venue for more 21st-century temporary exhibitions, usually included in the ticket price. (☏ 291 229 761; Rua da Mouraria 31; admission €2; ☉ 10am-6pm Tue-Sun)

Madeira Explorers   HIKING

19 ◎ MAP P48, A5

One of the best companies running levada hikes and other walks across the island. Hotel pick-up and drop-off included in the price. (☏ 291 763 701; www.madeira-levada-walks.com; 1st fl, Shop 23, Monumental Lido, Estrada Monumental; half-/full-day €27/37)

Tukxi   TOURS

20 ◎ MAP P48, E3

Tukxi uses a fleet of 10 electric Ape Calessinos – essentially tuk-tuks – to zip visitors around Funchal on a variety of tours led by very knowledgeable driver-guides. An innovative and eco-friendly way to see the city. (☏ 917 229 193; www.tukxi.pt; Rua dos Aranhas 53; tours from €25 per tuk tuk)

Eating

Regional Flavours   MADEIRAN $$

21 ✗ MAP P48, E3

Take a superb location on pedestrianised Rua da Carreira, a team plucked from top Madeiran restaurants and an inspired owner, and the result is one of the most authentic dining experiences in the archipelago. João Caldeira has a created a restaurant with perfect service, meticulous attention to detail and 100% Madeiran dishes using island-sourced ingredients as far as possible. (☏ 291 605 779; Rua da Carreira 146; mains €14.50-20; ☉ noon-9.30pm Mon-Sat, from 6pm Sun; ♿)

Il Gallo d'Oro   MEDITERRANEAN $$$

22 ✗ MAP P48, A5

Two Michelin stars shine brightly from the kitchen of chef Benoît Sinthon, who supplies very well-heeled diners with aromatic Mediterranean and gourmet Madeiran fare at the award-winning Cliff Bay Hotel. The renovated interior is surprisingly plain but the views make up for this. Smart casual attire required (jacket for men). (☏ 291 707 700; www.ilgallodoro.com; Cliff Bay Hotel, Estrada Monumental 147; menus €130-245, wine pairing €67-105; ☉ 7-9.30pm)

Armazém do Sal   PORTUGUESE $$

23 ✗ MAP P48, H4

Housed in an old stone-and-dark-beamed salt store, this is one of the city centre's best restaurants with a different menu to most of its competitors. Lamb and black pork are more mainland than Madeira, but scabbardfish and a dessert of pineapple carpaccio brings you right back to the Atlantic's sun-kissed shores. (☏ 291 241 285; www.

armazemdosal.com; Rua da Alfândega 135; mains €10-25; ⊙noon-3pm & 6.30-11pm Mon-Sat, 6.30-11pm Sun)

Dona Amélia
MEDITERRANEAN $$

24 ✖ MAP P48, B6

This little piece of elegant old Funchal has somehow survived amid the expanding concrete of this part of the Hotel Zone, offering Michelin-reviewed but affordable Mediterranean and Madeiran dishes in an oasis of traditional service. Some tables have wonderful Atlantic views. (☎291 225 784; www.donaameliarestaurant.com; Rua Imperatriz Dona Amélia 83; mains €10.50-17.50; ⊙6.30-11pm)

Boho Bistrô
BISTRO $$$

25 ✖ MAP P48, E4

Fusion isn't a word used often in Madeiran dining (bananas don't fuse that well), but this funky little urban bistro is attempting something never before tried on the island, and that is to marry traditional Madeiran/Portuguese flavours with their Asian and South American cousins. Add a contemporary design inserted into a traditional building and the effect is impressive. (☎918 048 432; www.boho.pt; Rua dos Aranhas 48/50; mains €20.50-23.50; ⊙12.30-3pm & 7pm until last customer)

O Avô
MADEIRAN $

26 ✖ MAP P48, H4

Outside the tables are dressed in traditional Madeiran stripes,

inside Europe's largest collection of football scarves hangs from the ceiling while 1000 beer bottles are lined up in glass cases. Characterful owner Ricardo has packed this ancient stone house in the backstreets of old Funchal with his personal collections, which you can admire as you enjoy the limited but well-cooked menu. (Rua da Praia 49; mains €7-11; ⊙8.30am-11pm Mon-Fri, from 11am Sat, 11am-5pm Sun; 🛜)

Quinta da Casa Branca
INTERNATIONAL $$$

27 ✖ MAP P48, A5

For a bit of olde-worlde elegance, head to the dining room of this *quinta* hotel, all Turkish carpets, antique lamps and starched tablecloths. Venison carpaccio, herring caviar and duck in gooseberry sauce are a continent away from usual Madeiran favourites, but the fare here provides a welcome change for those lingering longer in the Atlantic. Smart casual attire only. (☎291 700 770; www.quintacasabranca.pt; Rua da Casa Branca 7; mains €15-25; ⊙7-10.30pm)

A Confeitaria
BAKERY $

28 ✖ MAP P48, C5

This superb busy bakery with waiter service, opposite the casino, sells cakes and pastries all produced on the premises, plus coffees for €1. Freshness and reasonable prices attract hungry locals to the spartanly funky

Transatlantic Pit Stop

Before air travel, Madeira was a kind of staging post en route to points elsewhere for those travelling by ship across the Atlantic. Captain Cook called in here on one of his voyages of discovery, as did Darwin en route to the Galapagos Islands. Napoleon, however, possibly doesn't quite qualify as a visitor. In August 1815, on the way to exile on St Helena, he was kept aboard the HMS Northumberland docked in Funchal Bay – in the warming company of 600 bottles of Madeira wine (a gift from the British consul, it should be added).

The island's two most celebrated visitors came after the two world wars – Austrian Emperor Karl I arrived in exile in 1918, but pneumonia meant he never left. Churchill came to ease his depressive state in 1950 but left quickly after one oil painting and a bottle of Napoleon's wine.

Reid's Palace keeps a special book of illustrious guests, though you really have to be someone to deserve an entry – just 78 have made it onto the list in almost 130 years.

---

interior and the pavement tables outside, and goodies are available for takeaway. (Quinta Victoria, Avenida Do Infante; pastries from €0.70; ☺7am-9pm Mon-Fri, from 7.30am Sat & Sun; ☎)

Casa Madeirense

MADEIRAN $$

29 MAP P48, A5

A Hotel Zone original that predates most of what's around it, this delightfully kitschsy Madeiran restaurant set in an ancient stone house is tastefully done out in Camacha wicker, *azulejos* (hand-painted tiles), wine barrels and vivid Madeiran cloth. The purely regional menu of classic island meat and fish can be enjoyed in one of the cool, low-lit dining spaces. (☏291 766 700; www.casamadeirense-funchal. com; Estrada Monumental 153; mains €13-22; ☺11am-2am)

O Celeiro

MADEIRAN $$

30 MAP P48, E4

One of Funchal's oldest places to fill the hole, 'the barn' tries to live up to its name with rural knick-knackery adorning the walls, but is otherwise a tightly packed, traditionally tiled-and-beamed Madeiran restaurant. The menu covers fish and seafood, as well as a few random dishes such as pork in curry sauce and lamb chops. (☏291 230 622; www.restaurante oceleiro.com; Rua dos Aranhas 22; mains €12-21; ☺noon-3pm & 6-11pm Mon-Sat)

Bolo de Mel

Invariably described as 'honey cake', the dark-brown wheels of cake known as *bolo de mel* are actually made with molasses *(mel de cana)*. Eaten by Madeirans most often at Christmas, but by tourists year round, *bolo de mel* should never be cut, but torn into small chunks. It's often served as an accompaniment to Madeira wine.

Londres

SEAFOOD $$

31 MAP P48, F3

One of the original tourist restaurants around since 1976, the 'London' has a bright, simple no-frills dining room where you can enjoy the classics of Madeiran cuisine plus shellfish, calamari and other non-native dishes. The service is excellent and another good sign is that it's always packed with locals, especially at lunchtime. (Rua da Carreira 64A; mains €6-13.50; ⏰11.45am-3.45pm & 6-10.30pm; ❄)

Restaurante dos Combatentes

MADEIRAN $$

32 MAP P48, F3

No-nonsense, family-run option at one corner of the Jardim Municipal serving scabbardfish, *espetada* (barbecued beef on a skewer), lots of seafood and a couple of tasty vegetarian dishes. The simple dining room is adorned with a few antiques and rural-looking knick-knacks, but otherwise the focus is on honestly prepared local food. (📞291 223 388; cnr Ruas de San Francisco & Ivens; mains €10-21; ⏰11.45am-3.30pm & 6-10.30pm)

Hamburgueria do Mercado

DINER $

33 MAP P48, F3

Humongous gourmet burgers are the dining attraction at this joint. The interior is all white gloss and turquoise wallpaper and the staff are very friendly. You could attempt the Mercado burger, a huge slab of beef oozing with five different cheeses, or go for something lighter. (📞925 059 715; Rua da Carreira 75A; burgers €6.50-8; ⏰noon-11pm; 📶)

Grand Cafe Penha D'Águia

CAFE $

34 MAP P48, G4

This cafe, surely Funchal's most ostentatious, sits in a very prominent position smack-bang on the seafront. It may say 1844 on the sign, but this opulent place, all gold chandeliers and champagne buckets, is a 2018 addition. Skip the overpriced cakes and snacks inside for a cone of ice cream from its corner 'gelateria'. (Rua Das Comunidades Madeirenses 9; snacks from €3; ⏰8.30am-11.45pm; 📶)

Drinking

Reid's Tea Terrace TEAHOUSE

35 🚇 MAP P48, A5

The quintessential British–Madeiran experience is afternoon tea at Reid's. Some 24 types of tea, as well as cucumber sandwiches, delicate cakes and Champagne, are served on the terrace looking out over the bay of Funchal. Reservations are recommended. (📞291 717 171; www.belmond.com; Estrada Monumental 139; per person €35; ⏱3-4.30pm)

Vespas CLUB

36 🚇 MAP P48, D5

Madeira's top nightclub has been around since 1980 and was once the only place on the island for a proper night out. It's still the funnest, funkiest nightspot in these parts and often does its bit for the many festivals that take place in Funchal, such as Carnaval and the Festa da Flor. (📞291 234 800; www.vespas.pt; Avenida Sá Carneiro 7; ⏱11pm-7am Fri & Sat)

Golden Gate Cafe CAFE

37 🚇 MAP P48, G4

Having been around since 1841, the Golden Gate is one of Funchal's best-known cafes, though the place lost its olde-worlde charm in a glitzy refurb a few years ago. Skip the expensive food for a coffee or cocktail on the cobbles and watch the tourists file by. (📞291 234 383; Avenida Arriaga 21; ⏱8am-midnight)

Golden Gate Cafe

Copacabana
CLUB

Some claim that this club within the casino (see 47 ⭐ Map p48, D5) is Funchal's best night out. Music from the '80s and '90s, a resident DJ, regular live acts from Brazil, Madeira and Portugal, screen projections and a sometimes *very* mixed crowd make this one of the liveliest spots in the Atlantic to be when the sun goes down. (www.casinodamadeira.com; Avenida do Infante; ⏰11pm-3am Thu, to 4am Fri & Sat)

Cafe do Teatro
CAFE

This stylish cafe attached to the Teatro Baltazar Dias (see 46 ⭐ Map p48, F4) is open all day but really comes into its own after dark. Choose from a people-watching spot on the street or the courtyard where DJs pump out the latest sounds on a Saturday night. (Avenida Arriaga; ⏰10am-late; 📶)

Loja do Chá
TEAHOUSE

38 🚍 MAP P48, G4

More than a hundred teas are available at this tiny tearoom, whose tables spill out onto sunny Praça do Colombo. Snacks and light lunches accompany the green, black, jasmine and fruit infusions, some on the rather pricey end of the tea scale. (☎291 221 309; www.lojadochamadeira.com; Rua do Sabão 33-35; ⏰9.30am-7.30pm)

Cafe do Museu
CAFE

39 🚍 MAP P48, G3

Lurking in the loggia of the Museu de Arte Sacra, this is the

Beerhouse (p62)

Cristiano Ronaldo

As you will soon notice on Madeira, Funchal has given the world its best soccer player – ever, some claim. Cristiano Ronaldo dos Santos Aveiro was born in 1985 in the Funchal suburb of Santo António, north of the city centre. It's said his parents, working-class Funchalese, named him after president Reagan. He began his career at Andorinha, a fifth-tier club in Santo António but was soon on his way to Nacional and from there to Sporting Lisbon, Manchester United, Real Madrid and in 2018 Juventus. Ronaldo has achieved pretty much all there is to achieve in his sport, even winning the European Championship with Portugal in 2016. He has won the Ballon d'Or an amazing five times as well as the UEFA Champions League, the English Premier League and La Liga.

But for all his fame, he certainly hasn't forgotten the island in the Atlantic where it all started – he has donated many of his trophies, signed shirts and other soccer memorabilia to enable the creation of the Museu CR7, now a major Funchal tourist attraction. He's also a regular visitor to Madeira, his mother still lives here, and he can often be seen pulling up his shirt after scoring a goal to reveal an undershirt bearing the single word 'Madeira' daubed in marker pen.

museum's excellent cafe by day, but after dark it turns into a nightspot, especially at the weekends. Saturday brunch (€8) is particularly popular. (📞291 620 510; Praça do Município; 🕑10am-11pm Mon-Thu, to midnight Fri & Sat)

Penha D'Águia
CAFE

40 🚇 MAP P48, G3

Funchal's top chain of bakeries has been milling coffee beans and blackening the surfaces of *pastel de nata* since 1844, and its neatly designed cafes are arguably the best on the island. This branch breaks the mould with a dramatic interior of white and blue, with the odd retro element giving that perfect 21st-century look. (Rua de João Gago 6-8; 🕑7.30am-9pm Mon-Sat, from 8.30am Sun)

Mini Eco Bar
BAR

41 🚇 MAP P48, G4

Titchy, micro-space bar created as ecologically as possible (eco-friendly paints, A-rated electrical appliances), which really comes alive at weekends when DJs pump out cool tunes for a chilled audience. A great nightspot for hanging out with the crowd, though not if you want to sit down. (www.fresh-citrus.com; Rua de Alfândega 3; 🕑10pm-4am Wed-Sat; 🛜)

Beerhouse
MICROBREWERY

42 MAP P48, F5

The conspicuous assemblage of tent-roofed structures overlooking the marina is Funchal's only microbrewery, pumping out a decent German-style lager to go with a typical Madeiran tourist menu. It's spoilt slightly by the burly banana-farmer waiters being trussed up in Bavarian garb, but the beer, cocktails and swish location make it worth a shot. (291 229 011; www.beerhouse.pt; Pontão De São Lazaro; 10am-midnight Sun-Thu, to 2am Fri & Sat)

Pub No 2
PUB

43 MAP P48, A6

Housed in a traditional low Madeiran building, now overshadowed on all sides by glass-and-steel hotel edifices, Pub No 2 has been around forever and still serves a mixed bunch of expats and tourists in its low-lit, faux-English half-timbered spaces. Nice oasis in the Hotel Zone with English beers, food and footy on the box. (291 230 676; Rua do Favilla; 10am-2am;)

Prince Albert Pub
PUB

44 MAP P48, B6

Now loomed over by the new Savoy, Funchal's longest-established British pub has sports TV, Sunday roasts, occasional live music and a low-lit interior – expect lots of loud expat banter and British ale. (Rua Imperatriz Dona Amélia 86; 11am-midnight;)

Entertainment

Scat Funchal Jazz Club
JAZZ

45 MAP P48, A5

This superb little club near the Lido has nightly live music, a wonderful outdoor seating area from which to watch the Atlantic sunset, and frequent jam sessions. One of the last places to close in the Hotel Zone and a commendable dinner menu. (965 734 265; www.scatfunchalmusicclub.com; Promenade do Lido; 4pm-2am)

Fado Music

Though it didn't originate on the island, Madeirans share a love of fado music with their mainland cousins and Funchal has at least two places where you can hear it. With roots going back to early-19th-century Portugal, fado is voice and guitar music, often with a mournful, wistful sound and melancholic lyrics describing poverty, loss, longing and life at sea. Its origins are unclear but it has become the signature sound of the Portuguese-speaking world, along with the contrastingly upbeat samba.

Teatro Baltazar Dias   THEATRE

46 ⭐ MAP P48, F4

Funchal's grand, late-19th-century main theatre (there were once five!) is the place to head for high-brow entertainment, including classical music, fado, ballet and other performing arts, as well as film festivals and other events. (☎ 291 215 130; Avenida Arriaga; ⏲ ticket office 9am-5.30pm Mon & Tue, to 9.30pm Wed-Sun)

Casino da Madeira   CASINO

47 ⭐ MAP P48, D5

This concrete brutalist-style casino was designed by Oscar Niemeyer, the architect behind Brazil's planned capital Brasilia, and is a great night out even if you're not a gambler. Follow up the ritzy dinner and show by watching others fritter away their holiday money at the slot machines, or with a jig in the Copacabana (p60) disco. Smart casual attire recommended. (☎ 291 140 424; www.casinodamadeira.com; Avenida do Infante; ⏲ 3pm-3am Sun-Thu, 4pm-4am Fri & Sat; 🛜)

English Church   CONCERT VENUE

48 ⭐ MAP P48, E3

Funchal's large English Church, the epicentre of British expat life, seems to be used more for live music and various other events than for Christian worship. There's something on here at least once a week, with jazz, fado, chamber music and voice recitals regularly featuring on the programme. Check the website for details. (☎ 291 222 334; www.holytrinitychurchmadeira.com; Rua do Quebra Costas 18)

Shopping

Saudade Madeira   ARTS & CRAFTS

49 🔒 MAP P48, G3

Local producers of handicrafts and speciality foodstuffs pay for shelf space at this arty shop-cafe bang in the centre of Funchal. Everything from Madeira-themed paintings to locally made *azulejos* (hand-painted tiles) and T-shirts to driftwood art adorns the walls – all unique souvenir material. The cafe sells only Madeiran fare and the owners run various workshops in the basement.

There's live jazz Thursday to Saturday nights at 7.30pm. (☎ 291 237 151; www.facebook.com/saudademadeira; Rua João Gago 2; ⏲ 10am-7pm Mon-Wed, to midnight Thu-Sat)

Livraria Esperança   BOOKS

50 🔒 MAP P48, G2

This huge shop selling secondhand and new books fills an entire palace and claims to stock more than 100,000 titles, making it Portugal's largest. Most of the books are in Portuguese but there is a foreign-language section. It's a great place to pick up obscure books on Madeiran history, natural history and the like, plus guidebooks and maps. (www.livraria-esperanca.pt; Rua dos Ferreiros 119 & 156; ⏲ 9am-7pm Mon-Fri)

Fábrica Ribeiro Sêco   FOOD

51 🔒 MAP P48, A3

The Fábrica Ribeiro Sêco has re-
vived some of the sugar-processing
traditions that once made Madeira
wealthy. Buy the island's famous
molasses, *bolo de mel* (molasses
cake), sugar-cane biscuits and
recipe books at the factory, located
to the north of the city centre.
Otherwise they are available in
supermarkets across the island.
(📞 291 741 503; www.fabricaribeiroseco.
com; Rua das Maravilhas 170; ⏰9am-
1pm & 2-6pm Mon-Fri)

La Vie   MALL

52 🔒 MAP P48, E4

This 21st-century mall is the best
shopping centre between Lisbon
and New York. In addition to the
big-name shops, it also has a
pharmacy, a large supermarket,
cash machines and mobile-phone
dealerships. (📞 291 215 420; https://
funchal.lavieshopping.pt; Rua Dr Brito
Câmara 9; ⏰9am-10pm)

Forum Madeira   MALL

53 🔒 MAP P48, A5

If you are staying in one of the
many hotels or self-catering flats
located at the western end of the
Hotel Zone, you will at some point
gravitate towards this immensely
useful shopping centre with its
Pingo Doce supermarket, cafes,
sports and outdoor shop and cin-
ema. (📞291 706 825; www.forum
madeira.com; Estrada Monumental

390; ⏰9am-11pm Sun-Thu, to midnight Fri & Sat)

Fabrica Santo Antonio   FOOD

54 🔒 MAP P48, G3

A delightfully old-fashioned shop,
with its early 20th-century display
cases, scales and counters still in
place, from which staff offer the
classic made-in-Madeira tooth-
rotters such as brightly packaged
bolo de mel (molasses cake; p58),
sugar-cane biscuits and traditional jams. (📞291 220 255; www.
fabricastoantonio.com; Travessa do
Forno 27-29; ⏰9am-7pm Mon-Fri, to
1pm Sat)

Madeira Shopping   MALL

55 🔒 MAP P48, A3

Madeira's largest shopping mall,
situated high above the city centre
in the Santo António neighbourhood. There are more than 100
shops, plus restaurants and a large
supermarket. Take bus 8A. (www.
madeirashopping.pt; Caminho de Santa
Quitéria 45; ⏰9am-11pm Sun-Thu, to
midnight Fri & Sat)

Artecouro   FASHION & ACCESSORIES

56 🔒 MAP P48, G4

This small, unmarked emporium
sells leather goods made from the
finest Portuguese hides in Funchal,
including belts, handbags, brief-
cases and wallets. (Rua da Alfândega
15; ⏰10am-1.20pm & 3-7pm Mon-Fri,
10am-1.20pm Sat)

Livraria Esperança (p63)

Santa Luzia Flea Market

MARKET

Every last Sunday of the month a flea market takes place at the Jardim de Santa Luzia (see 10 ◎ Map p48, F1) . There's all sorts of bric-a-brac on sale, including secondhand Madeiran embroidery, yesteryear souvenirs and island succulents. (Jardim de Santa Luzia; ⊘8am-6pm last Sun of the month)

O Bordão

SPORTS & OUTDOORS

57 🔒 MAP P48, F4

Lost your compass or forgotten your hiking boots? Head for O Bordão (The Staff), the island's only dedicated outdoor gear shop. The range is limited and prices aren't exactly low, but it's just the place to solve a kit emergency. (Galerias de São Lourenço, Loja 35, Avenida Arriaga 41-43; ⊘10am-7pm Mon-Fri, to 1pm Sat)

Explore ◈
East Funchal

East Funchal is all about the Zona Velha, an old fishers' neighbourhood that until recently was a rundown and almost lifeless area. Today it's been transformed into a hip quarter packed with bars, galleries, shops and restaurants and is the place to head in Funchal come nightfall. The stellar attraction on the edge of the Zona Velha is the Mercado dos Lavradores, Funchal's vibrant market.

The Short List

○ **Zona Velha (p68)** *Exploring the once-derelict area of merchants' storehouses and fishermen's cottages, rejuvenated as a nightlife and dining hotspot.*

○ **Mercado dos Lavradores (p70)** *Browsing Madeira's main market, overflowing with colour and fragrant with flowers, fish and fruit.*

○ **Jardins Botânicos da Madeira (p72)** *Enjoying the Atlantic's finest set of gardens with its cacti, parrots and multi-hued shrubs.*

○ **Venda da Donna Maria (p79)** *Sampling authentic Madeiran meals made using granny's recipe book and served on her old crockery.*

○ **Arsenio's (p81)** *Relaxing with nights of grilled meat and wistful fado music in the cool Atlantic breeze.*

Getting There & Around

🚶 The vast majority of visitors explore East Funchal on foot. In fact the Zona Velha can only be seen in this way.

🚌 Some Horários do Funchal buses terminate on the edge of the Zona Velha.

East Funchal Map on p74

Top Experience 📷
Zona Velha

Crammed between the Mercado dos Lavradores and the Fortaleza de Santiago, Funchal's 'Old Zone' is the most happening place on Madeira these days. A dilapidated area of abandoned 19th-century fisherfolks' cottages and merchants' houses just a few years ago, this neighbourhood of tightly packed streets has been transformed into Funchal's nightlife epicentre by the arrival of new and imaginative bars, restaurants and hostels.

◉ **MAP P74, C3**

Rua de Santa Maria & Rua D Carlos I

Rua de Santa Maria

No more than few metres wide, Funchal's funkiest street, Rua de Santa Maria, runs the entire length of the Zona Velha, its cobbles a car-free throng of tourists and locals from lunchtime to breakfast. By day it's almost blocked in places by the tables and chairs of some of Funchal's best restaurants; by night the crowds spill out of the tiny bars, *ponchas* (local sugar-cane spirit drink) and *caipirinhas* (the national cocktail of Brazil, made with *cachaça,* limes and sugar)in hand. There's also a lot of history in this street. Look for the diminutive 17th-century **Capela da Boa Viagem**, where the street intersects Rua de Boa Viagem, and the tall merchants' houses, their musty cellars harking back to the first settlers and Madeira's days as a place of Atlantic trade. This is also where you'll find the vast majority of the Zona Velha's street art, created as part of the Open Doors Arts Project.

Largo do Corpo Santo

Rua de Santa Maria widens out towards its eastern end into pretty Largo do Corpo Santo, where there are a couple of low-key attractions amid the touristy restaurants. The **Capela do Corpo Santo** is the old fisherfolks' chapel, though only the 15th-century portal is from the original building. The only section of Funchal's 16th-century city wall to have survived can also be found nearby.

Seafront

Gliding silently above the red-tiled roofs of the Zona Velha are the cabins of the Teleférico (cable car), its 21st-century glass-and-steel terminus the dominant feature of the Zone Velha seafront. At the other end is the **Jardim do Almirante Reis**, once a football pitch (hence the footballer statue) but now a place where tourists and Funchalese come to hang out.

★ **Top Tips**

o Try to explore the Zona Velha after dark when all the bars are open.

o The cable car from Monte takes you into the Zona Velha.

o The Jardim do Almirante Reis is a popular picnicking spot.

✕ **Take a Break**

Venda da Donna Maria (p79) is a superb halt for a Madeiran lunch.

Riso (p80) at the eastern end of the Zona Velha has Atlantic views and a light, rice-based menu.

Top Experience 📷

Mercado dos Lavradores

Bursting with exotic colour, heavy with wonderful mid-Atlantic aromas and busy from morning till late afternoon with a procession of shopping locals and curious tourists, Funchal's main market is one of the city's most captivating attractions. Built in 1940 by architect Edmundo Tavares, this art deco structure has retained the majority of its original features, including very high-quality azulejos (hand-painted tiles) from the mainland.

◎ MAP P74, B3

Largo dos Lavradores

⊘ 8am-7pm Mon-Thu, 7am-8pm Fri, 7am-2pm Sat

Flowers

The market's amazing colour begins right at the entrance where local women in folk costume sell all kinds of exotic flowers, shrubs, bulbs and seeds. Over the autumn and winter the Madeiran national flower, *estrelícia* (bird of paradise), is in bloom – a wonderfully striking choice if you're looking for cut flowers. Throughout the year, a whole array of weird and wonderful triffids is on display, including a selection of the island's famous orchids.

Fruit

For most visitors the fruit stalls around the open central courtyard are the real highlight. For every fruit you recognise, there'll be one nearby you don't. Those that grow on Madeira include *anone* (custard apples), *banana ananaz* (monstera), *tomate inglês* (tamarillo) and papaya, as well as, of course, the island's famous sweet miniature bananas. Other fruity treasures include ripe mangoes from Brazil, sweet oranges from the mainland and local grapes; prices are mostly comparable with the island's supermarkets.

Fish

Pass through the fruit market and up the steps for a grandstand view of Funchal's main fish market. The stars of the show here are the scary-looking *espada* (scabbardfish) – black, slippery, eel-like creatures with rows of razor-sharp teeth and huge watery eyes. They are the island's staple fish, caught at night deep below the surface of the Atlantic. Huge bloodied slabs of tuna also catch the eye, as does the nonchalant skill of the fishmongers as they fillet and hack their way through the day's catch.

★ Top Tips

o Get there early for the fish market – it's as good as over by lunchtime.

o The market now hosts various foodie and other events – check the tourist office calendar.

o Some of the vendors on the upper level are a bit pushy, but normally take no for an answer.

o Souvenirs at the market are a bit pricey as it attracts cruise-ship tours with limited time.

✗ Take a Break

Pau de Canela (p78) is the pick of the bunch of cafes that ring the market.

Top Experience 📷

Jardins Botânicos da Maderia

Covering 80,000 sq metres, rising from 150m to 300m above sea level and crammed with the most exotic collection of plant life in Europe, Madeira's main botanical garden is like few others. It teems with tourists who wander in amazement at the leafy spectacle on offer. Only created in the 1950s, it's one of Madeira's top tourist attractions.

◎ MAP P74, C1

📞 291 211 200

www.sra.pt

Caminho do Meio

admission €6

🕑 9am-6pm

🚌 31/31A

Fabulous Flora

There's so much to see here it's difficult to know where to start. Some of the highlights include the Madeiran indigenous and endemic species section, the area of succulents and cacti, the topiary section, the area devoted to medicinal and aromatic plants, the palm tree garden and the formal shrub garden mosaic – one of Madeira's top photo opportunities. Plants to look out for are the *estrelícia* (bird of paradise) that flowers in winter, the mammoth prickly pears with leaves like saw blades, the indigenous *Musschia aurea* with their triffid-like blossoms and the *Geranium maderense* that bursts like a firework in a shower of purple flowers.

Louro Parque

The neighbouring aviary at the southern end can be visited on the same ticket. Here parrots, parakeets, cockatoos, budgies, canaries and warblers squawk and chitter the day away in their spacious cages. The multi-coloured birds here are from every corner of the globe but most hail from South America. A colossal, ancient-looking turtle occupies the artificial pond around which some of the cages are arranged.

Hidden Corners

Away from the main areas, the gardens have many hidden corners that are worth seeking out. The Lover's Cave is a fern-lined rocky grotto with a table and chairs made of volcanic pebbles. The *miradouro* (lookout) has cracking views of the Bom Sucesso creek – controversially, however, the Via Rápida motorway actually tunnels its way just below the gardens, which spoils the effect somewhat. In another nook you'll discover a typical Santana A-frame house.

★ **Top Tips**

- All plants are labelled with scientific name, common name, family and country of origin.

- Feeding the birds in the Louro Parque is not permitted.

- Maps are located at strategic spots and explanations are in English.

- Due to the gardens' altitude, it's best not to visit during periods of bad weather as it is often cold and wet.

✕ **Take a Break**

The only place to take a break at the gardens is the **snack bar** (snacks €2-4; ⊙9am-5pm) on the northwest side.

For reviews see

◎ Top Experiences p69
◎ Experiences p75
✕ Eating p78
◻ Drinking p80
✦ Entertainment p81
◻ Shopping p82

0 ▲ 0
N
200 m
0.1 miles

6 ◉ 9

R de João de Deus

8 ◉ Museu Henrique e
Francisco Franco

IBTAM
Museum ◉ 7

3 ◉
Jardins Botânicos
da Madeira ▲

R Conde Carvalhal

R do Carmo

R do Visconde de Anadia

R do Brigadeiro Ouridol

R da Infanda

25 ◻

R do Hospital Velho

12 ✕

10 ◉ Museu do
Brinquedo

26 ◻
14 ✕
R Latino Coelho
R de Santa Maria

15 ✕
2 ◉
Madeira
Story
Centre

R José da Silva

R da Boa
Viagem
21 ✕

R D Carlos I

6 ◉
Casa da Luz–
Museu de
Electricidade

Lower Cable
Car Station

Jardim do
Almirante Reis

Zona ◉
Velha

13 ✕ 16 ✕
24 ◉
23 ◉
20 ◻
19 ◻

R Bela-São Tiago

28 ✕
R de Santa Maria
R de Santa Maria
R Portão de São Tiago
R D Carlos I

18 ◉

Igreja do
Socorro

22 ✕
5 ◉

17 ✕

Largo do
Socorro

Fortaleza de ◉ 4
Santiago

11 ✕

Mercado dos
Lavradores ◉

27 ◻

R Dr Fernão de Ornelas

1 ◉ 1 ◢

Praça da
Autonomia

R 31 de Janeiro

R 5 de Outubro

Av do Mar

Experiences

Miradouro do Pináculo

VIEWPOINT

1 ⊙ MAP P74, F2

Featuring in many a holiday brochure, the view from this *miradouro* (lookout) east of Funchal is unique as it looks slightly back at the city from the cliffs of São Gonçalo. Take bus 38 to Estalgem Montanha. (Rua Conde Carvalhal; ⊙24hr)

Madeira Story Centre

MUSEUM

2 ⊙ MAP P74, C3

This interactive museum tells Madeira's story in an easily digestible way, from the moment the first volcanic rock seethed through the Atlantic's waves to the tourism of the late 20th century. Highlights include a mock up of a rather peeved Napoleon being presented with Madeira wine aboard the HMS *Northumberland* en route to St Helena and a recreation of the Aquila Airlines flying boat cabin, with an interesting film on the service playing as in-flight entertainment. (☏291 639 082; www.madeirastorycentre.com; Rua Dom Carlos I 27-29; adult/concession €5/3; ⊙10am-6pm daily)

Jardins do Palheiro

GARDENS

3 ⊙ MAP P74, C1

Some 500m up in the hills east of Funchal, these much-loved subtropical gardens are a beautiful mix of formal and 'wild' areas with thousands of unusual and

Madeira Story Centre

familiar plants. After a good walk, retreat to the tearoom to refuel. Take bus 36A or 37. (www.palhei rogardens.com; Caminho da Quinta do Palheiro 32; adult/child €11/free; ⏰9am-5.30pm)

Fortaleza de Santiago FORTRESS

4 ⊙ MAP P74, E4

The ochre and dark-pink fortress that caps the Zona Velha seafront was built in the first half of the 17th century, when Funchal was vulnerable to pirate attacks. The complex is set to become Madeira's Archaeology Museum at some point in the coming years, but most of the fun here will still be about scrambling around the various rooms, turrets, battlements and hidden corners. Expect great photo ops. (Rua de Santa Maria; adult/concessions €3/1.50; ⏰9.30am-5.30pm Mon-Fri)

Igreja do Socorro CHURCH

5 ⊙ MAP P74, E4

This impressive clifftop church at the eastern end of the Zona Velha is a 1750 rebuild – the original was destroyed in the earthquake of 1748. Slightly off the tourist trail and looking out across the Atlantic in all its baroque pomp, it boasts some impressive *azulejos* (hand-painted tiles) and a painted ceiling atmospherically dulled by the smoke of a million candles. (Largo do Socorro; ⏰8.30am-6pm)

Casa da Luz – Museu de Electricidade MUSEUM

6 ⊙ MAP P74, B4

Decommissioned in 1989, Funchal's old power station – still the headquarters of EEM (Empresa de Electricidade da Madeira – Madeira Electric Company) – has been turned into

---

Door Art of the Zona Velha

Strolling through the Zona Velha, you cannot fail to notice the neighbourhood's weird and wonderful door art, created as part of the Projecto Arte Portas Abertas (Open Doors Arts Project; www. arteportasabertas.com). The idea to spice up the rather derelict doors and gates of the area is the brainchild of Spanish artist José Maria Zyberchema, who since 2011 has been inspiring local artists and arty locals to splash works of public art across the Zona Velha. The project has been credited with giving a huge lift to what was becoming a very rundown chunk of Funchal – a now quickly revitalising Zona Velha has become the nightlife hub of the Madeiran capital. The artist hopes the idea might spread to other communities across the island – some similar art can be seen on the old doors of Machico.

Madeira's Traditional Culture

One of the many pleasures to be sampled on Madeira is the island's traditional culture, always a vividly colourful experience. There's a lot to see year-round across the island, from embroidery demonstrations and folk dancing in the streets of Funchal to food fairs and tasting sessions in ancient wineries.

Folk dancing has become more accessible in recent years as more hotels and restaurants host performances. Dancers normally don the Madeiran folk costume for the occasion (baggy trousers, white shirt and goat-skin shepherd's boots for the men; traditional striped cloth dress and white blouse for women). Both sexes pop a *carapuca* on their heads – a black pointed skullcap. Songs are warbled to the accompaniment of the *rajão* or *braguinha* (a kind of mandolin), a drum, castanets and a *raspadeiro* (a notched stick played like a washboard). Singers bash the ground with a *brinquinho* – a jangling stick of puppets and small bells.

Wicker and embroidery are the two main traditional handicrafts, but there are of course other, smaller-scale industries. Cottage jewellery production has taken off in recent years and items are available from stalls in the Armazém do Mercado (p82) and from Saudade Madeira (p63).

a museum dedicated to the history of electricity generation on the island and to electricity itself. Downstairs a huge hall holds the old diesel generators but the fun really starts upstairs, where you'll find many interactive, electricity-related exhibits. (Rua Casa da Luz 2; adult/child €2.70/free; ⏰10am-12.30pm & 2-6pm Tue-Sat; 👬)

IBTAM Museum MUSEUM

7 ◉ MAP P74, B1

IBTAM is the organisation that oversees Madeiran embroidery production – anything bearing their hologram label is guaranteed to be the genuine,

locally made article. This quaint museum at IBTAM's headquarters examines many aspects of traditional embroidery with mock-ups of 19th-century rooms awash with embroidered textiles. A film at the end of the exhibition looks at the island's traditional industries and IBTAM's role. (Rua Visconde de Anadia 44; admission €2.50; ⏰9.30am-12.30pm & 2-5.30pm Mon-Fri)

Museu Henrique e Francisco Franco GALLERY

8 ◉ MAP P74, B1

The works of early-20th-century Funchal sculptor Francisco

Franco can be found at this small museum, which also displays works by his painter brother. (📞291 211 090; Rua João de Deus 13; admission free; ⏰9.30am-6pm Mon-Fri)

Quinta da Boa Vista GARDENS

9 ◉ MAP P74, F1

Founded by a former Honorary British Consul Cecil Garton, this garden is the best place to experience Madeira's exquisite orchids. The orchid houses are a riot of *Cattleyas*, *Cymbidiums* and *Paphiopedilums* but the rest of the place could do with a tidy round. (📞291 220 468; Rua Lombo da Boa Vista; admission Feb-May/Jun-Jan €4.50/2.50; ⏰9am-5pm Mon-Sat)

Museu do Brinquedo MUSEUM

10 ◉ MAP P74, B3

This toy museum occupies seven rooms at the Armazém do Mercado and is essentially made up of the 20,000-piece private collection of one José Manuel Borges Pereira. More for parents than kids, it's an I-used-to-have-one-of-those-in-the-seventies sort of experience with everything from Corgi and Dinky cars to Action Man and Star Wars figures on display. The museum possesses Madeira's only train set layout and often puts on free themed exhibitions in other parts of the Armazém do Mercado. (www.armazemdomercado.com/museu; 2nd fl, Armazém do Mercado, Rua Hospital Velho 28; adult/child €5/3; ⏰10am-6pm Mon-Fri, to 2pm Sat; 🚻)

Eating

Pau de Canela CAFE $

11 ✖ MAP P74, B3

Old-skool bakery-cafe next to the Mercado dos Lavradores, usually inhabited by working-class Funchalese families, market workers and the odd pigeon, all of whom come to feed on cheap pastries, cakes, pizzas, made-in-front-of-you sandwiches and toasties. The most expensive item on the menu costs €2. The decor is pure late-20th century. (Rua Latino Coelho 10; snacks €0.50-2; ⏰7am-8pm Mon-Fri, to 1pm Sat)

The Snug INTERNATIONAL $

12 ✖ MAP P74, B2

Minimalist, hip and innovative, this recently renamed bar-cafe at the entrance to the Armazém do Mercado is a great place for a bite to eat after perusing the stalls of the market. It's also good for a beer at the weekends as local DJs spin their stuff. (Armazém do Mercado, Rua Hospital Velho 28; mains €3-5; ⏰9.30am-8pm Mon-Thu & Sat, to midnight Fri, to 6pm Sun; 🛜)

Gavião Novo SEAFOOD $$

13 ✖ MAP P74, C3

Madeira's top seafood restaurant is an intimate affair at the heart of the Zona Velha, attracting tourists, locals and Portuguese

PURPLE MARBLES MADEIRA/ALAMY STOCK PHOTO ©

Museu Henrique e Francisco Franco (p77)

rich and famous, who come for one of the most authentic dining experiences on the island. Fish from the waters around Madeira are complemented by Portuguese seafood air-freighted in every Satuday. Desserts are made fresh twice a day and only the best Portuguese olive oils are used. (☎291 229 238; www.gaviaonovo.pt; Rua Santa Maria 131; mains €8-17; ☺noon-11pm)

Venda da Donna Maria MADEIRAN $$

14 ✖ MAP P74, B3

This great shabby-chic Zona Velha restaurant uses local recipes that every Funchal *avozinha* (granny) would instantly recognise. Take a seat at the tightly packed

jumble of tables to enjoy *espada* (scabbardfish) with banana, São Martinho codfish and lots of other genuine Madeiran favourites. To find out what's in your meal, see the recipes writ large on the walls.

For even more intimate dining, phone ahead to book the amusingly named *confessionário* (confessional) table tucked into a cosy basalt alcove. (☎291 621 225; Rua de Santa Maria 51; mains €12-20; ☺11am-11.30pm)

Tasca Literária MADEIRAN $$

15 ✖ MAP P74, C3

The slightly obscure theme here is famous visitors to Madeira (mostly Portuguese celebs), but with a blood-red and basalt interior and black-and-white photos covering the walls it's an atmospheric place to spend an evening in the Zona Velha. Plates come laden with honestly prepared portions of *espada* (scabbardfish), tuna, rabbit, goat and lamb, and the wine flows freely.

Reservations advised Friday and Saturday evenings. (📞291 220 348; Rua de Santa Maria 77; mains €9-21; 🕐11am-11pm; 📶)

Santa Maria
INTERNATIONAL $$

16 MAP P74, C3

This snazzy, minimalist restaurant belonging to a great Zona Velha hostel serves up lobster, fish burgers, local limpets and sushi on square plates. The bar is made of sardine cans, the lightbulbs are bare, the staff efficient and the courtyard out back an oasis of peace when the party gets going on Rua de Santa Maria. (www.santamariafunchal.com; Rua de Santa Maria 145; mains €14-19; 🕐11am-midnight; 📶)

English Menus 💬

We have yet to find a place to eat on Madeira that didn't have an English menu, or one in German, French, Spanish and even Finnish for that matter, though translations can be a bit ropey and sometimes amusing. Very few waiters have problems communicating in English, even in the remotest of places.

Riso
INTERNATIONAL $$

17 ❌ MAP P74, E4

The menu at this restaurant abutting the Fortaleza de Santiago is a rice-themed trip around the world. Every dish (even the desserts) contains basmati, Thai, arborio, wild or venere. All seats have unobstructed Atlantic vistas, meaning you may linger longer over your risotto than you originally intended. (www.riso-fx.com; Rua de Santa Maria; mains €6-13; 🕐noon-2.30pm & 7-10.30pm Tue-Sun)

Drinking

Madeira Rum House
BAR

18 🍺 MAP P74, E4

Offering Madeira's own rum, the William Hinto brand, this is a superb addition to the Zona Velha drinking scene. The smooth tipple in question is made using the island's cane sugar and fermented in oak casks. A bottle makes a very authentic souvenir. (📞291 611 303; Rua Portão de São Tiago 19C; 🕐6pm-midnight)

Venda Velha
BAR

19 🍺 MAP P74, D3

This bar-restaurant attempts to recreate the shop-taverns of the early 20th century, once the community hubs across the island. Special focus here falls on Madeiran *poncha* (sugar-cane spirit drink), a more boozy drink than many non-Madeirans imagine –

head there after midnight to see what we mean. (☎914 758 975; Rua de Santa Maria 170; ⏱4pm-1am Sun-Thu, to 2am Fri & Sat)

Mercearia da Poncha BAR

20 🚇 MAP P74, D3

Specialising in Madeiran *poncha* (sugar-cane spirit drink), this small Zona Velha bar often crams Rua de Santa Maria with drinkers until the early hours. A lively atmosphere is always guaranteed. (Rua de Santa Maria 154; ⏱5pm-1am Tue-Sun)

23 Vintage Bar CLUB

21 🚇 MAP P74, B3

Celebrating the music of the 1960s to 1990s, this great little club-bar livens up weekends in the Zona Velha. Friday nights are all about paying nostalgic tribute to an iconic band or artist such as Modern Talking, Kylie Minogue, Lenny Kravitz or U2; more eclectic Saturdays are normally jukebox night. (Rua de Santa Maria 23; ⏱8pm-2am Fri & Sat)

Barreirinha Cafe BAR

22 🚇 MAP P74, F4

Outside-only cafe-bar above the *complexo balnear* (swimming complex) at the eastern end of the Zona Velha offering snacks and drinks to the sound of brine on basalt at any time of day. Weekend DJs and a real mixed crowd. (Largo do Socorro 1; ⏱8am-midnight Sun-Thu, to 2am Fri & Sat)

Madeiran Coffee

Forget espressos and lattes, the bean-crazed Portuguese have their own words for their brews. A *bica* is a shot of coffee – an espresso; a *garoto* is 50% espresso, 50% milk. A *chinesa* is a strong milky coffee, while a *carioca* is a weak espresso. A *galão* is as close to a latte as you're going to get and is served in a tall glass. Alternatively you could just have a good ole cuppa *chá* (tea).

Entertainment

Sabor e Fado LIVE MUSIC

23 ⭐ MAP P74, D3

Though not as illustrious as other Funchal fado-and-dinner venues, Sabor e Fado is an intimate affair. The menu is meat-heavy; the live music starts at 7pm and the staff often get in on the act. Fado nights are dinner-and-music events – pay for food at a table, and the music is free. (☎925 612 259; Travessa das Torres 10; ⏱6pm-1am Thu-Tue)

Arsenio's LIVE MUSIC

24 ⭐ MAP P74, D3

The aroma of a loaded charcoal grill wafts along Rua de Santa Maria from Arsenio's, luring evening strollers into the old, atmospheric dining room, all basalt floors, ancient beams and leather chairs. Every evening from 7pm to 11pm, meals are taken with a dose of fado, Arsenio's being the best place on Madeira to experience Portugal's signature musical genre. Book ahead for the best seats. (☑291 224 007; Rua de Santa Maria 169; ⊘noon-late)

Shopping

Patrício & Gouveia
GIFTS & SOUVENIRS

25 🏛 MAP P74, B2

Funchal's classiest souvenir emporium is a world away from the bird-of-paradise-flower fridge magnets and Chinese T-shirts of the Hotel Zone. This venerable institution brings together the finest handicrafts and foodstuffs Madeira has to offer, with the company's own embroidery the star of the show. Has the longest lunch break of any shop in Madeira. (☑291 222 723; www.patriciogouveia.pt; Rua Visconde de Anadia 34; ⊘9am-1pm & 3-6.30pm Mon-Fri, to noon Sat)

Lillie Ceramics
CERAMICS

26 🏛 MAP P74, B3

Thrown, fired, glazed and sold in this shop run by two Finnish sisters, the ceramics on sale here sport delicate, Madeira-themed motifs, most of a floral ilk. Prices range from €4.50 to €130 with everything from small cups to huge platters and jugs on display. All items can be shipped. (☑914 486 951; Armazém do Mercado, Rua Latino Coelho 39; ⊘10am-7pm Mon-Fri, to 2pm Sat)

Armazém do Mercado
MARKET

Exquisitely renovated by architect Paul David, the man behind Calheta's Casa das Mudas, this old embroidery factory and mechanic's shop (see 10 ⊙ Map p74, B3) has been transformed into an urban pop-up space for local businesses and craftsmen. It also houses the Museu do Brinquedo (p78) and a couple of hip eateries. (www.armazemdomercado.com; Rua Hospital Velho 28 & Rua Latino Coelho 39; ⊘10am-8pm Mon-Sat)

Responsible Retail

Over the past decade and a half, Funchal has witnessed a retail boom, the most tangible evidence of which are the large shopping malls that have been planted at strategic points. While these glitzy consumer temples offer welcome convenience, they have put in doubt the future of many of the city centre's old family-run, been-there-forever shops that are a delight to explore. Supporting these often wonderfully old-fashioned emporia may help them to survive in the face of an onslaught of chains and outlets, thus preserving the character of Funchal's city centre.

Patrício & Gouveia

Bordal
ARTS & CRAFTS

27 MAP P74, A2

Bordal is Madeira's top embroidery company, its mark (a hologram) a guarantee the item you are buying has been made on the island. The shop specialises in fine embroidered linens and the factory upstairs can also be visited free of charge. Women come here daily to pick up and drop off work that they complete at home. (291 222 965; www.bordal.pt; Rua Dr Fernão Ornelas 77; shop 9am-1pm & 2-7pm Mon-Fri, 9am-1pm Sat, factory to 6pm Mon-Fri)

Fabrica de Chapeus de Santa Maria
FASHION & ACCESSORIES

28 MAP P74, E4

Tiny, old, ramshackle Zona Velha workshop where traditional Madeiran hats are sewn together amid piles of headgear, ancient sewing machines and scraps of material. Hours are erratic. (Rua de Santa Maria 238-9; 11am-7pm Mon-Fri)

Top Experience 📷
Monte

Roosting high above Funchal, this aristocratic villa quarter was once the stomping ground of wealthy families who preferred summer's lower temperatures 500m up. Today it's one of Madeira's must-sees, with a cluster of sights interspersed with outlandish greenery and exotically perfumed air. Getting here on the cable car from the Zona Velha is also part of the fun.

🚠 From the Botanical Gardens and Zona Velha

🚌 Horários do Funchal service 21 to Largo da Fonte, 22 to Babosas or 48 from the Hotel Zone.

Igreja da Nossa Senhora

Some 68 stone steps (pictured left) climb dramatically to the doors of one of Madeira's finest churches, Monte's **Igreja da Nossa Senhora** (⊙services 6pm Tue, Wed, Fri & Sat, 8.30am Thu, 8am & 11am Sun). Rising in eye-balancing baroque symmetry, it was built in the wake of the 1748 earthquake that destroyed the original. The huge baroque altar bears the tiny statue of Our Lady, one of the most revered icons on the island. However a side chapel to the left as you enter attracts the most attention – it contains the tomb of exiled Austrian Emperor Karl I.

Toboggans in the Sun

Ernest Hemingway described it as the 'most exhilarating experience' of his life – whether he was attempting a little sarcasm, we'll never know, but nonetheless the **toboggan ride** (Carreiros do Monte; www.carreirosdomonte.com; Caminho do Monte; 10min ride for 2 people €30) down to Livramento is a must-do. Toboggans were once the only way goods could be carried across Madeira's steep and roadless landscapes and the Monte *carros de cesto* are a relic of those days. The toboggans are made of Camacha wicker with padded seats for two people. The drivers wear straw boater hats, white shirts, white trousers and shoes with rubber soles that help them brake the toboggan's plunge down the asphalt. Ten minutes of slithering for €30 (two people) may seem as steep as the slope you are descending, but it's a unique experience, if possibly not as exhilarating as Papa described it.

Railway Remnants

The only train to ever run on Madeira was a rack-and-pinion service that climbed 4km from the city centre to Monte and then on to Terreiro da Luta between 1893 and 1943. The

★ **Top Tips**

∘ Weather in Monte can differ enormously to the conditions down in Funchal.

∘ Services at the Igreja da Nossa Senhora take place Tuesday, Wednesday, Friday and Saturday at 6pm, Thursday at 8.30am and Sunday at 8am and 11am.

✕ **Take a Break**

Cafe do Parque (Largo da Fonte; snacks €1-9; ⊙9am-5pm) on Monte's atmospheric old square is a pretty spot for coffee and cakes.

The **Alto Monte** (Caminho das Tihas; mains €5-16; ⊙11am-11pm) cafe plays it safe with Madeiran favourites.

one-carriage train was a major tourist attraction (as the cable car is today), hauling wealthy tourists up from the city centre. However a couple of accidents and bankruptcy put paid to the service – all that's left of those days is the almost completely straight Via do Comboio (Train St) that follows the route of the tracks, a railway viaduct in Monte just off Largo da Fonte and Monte's old railway station, which stands in a forlorn state on the corner of the square, next to the road.

Monte Palace Tropical Gardens

One of the highlights of any visit to Monte is a wander around the **Monte Palace Tropical Gardens** (☏291 780 800; www.montepalace. com; Largo da Fonte; admission €12.50; ◷9.30am-6pm). This former hotel began life in the late 18th century as a private residence belonging to the British Consul Charles Murray. In the late 1980s it was purchased by local entrepreneur José Berardo who transformed it into a weird-and-wonderful tourist attraction by filling the grounds with fountains, grottoes, follies, sculpture pieces and lots of exotic plant life.

Teleféricos

The most interesting way to reach Monte is on the **cable car** (☏291 780 288; www.madeiracablecar.com; Jardim do Almirante Reis; ◷single/ return €11/16) from the Zona Velha, a major engineering project completed in 2000. The 20-minute ride above the red rooftops, banana

Monte Palace Tropical Gardens

The Last Habsburg

There's an unexpected historical full stop on the island of Madeira – a place that witnessed the last act of a centuries-old story, far away from its main central European stage. As every Austrian royalist knows, Monte is the final resting place of the last Habsburg, exiled Emperor of Austria and last king of Bohemia and Hungary – Karl I. But how did the final line in the story of the Habsburgs, a dynasty that dominated European royal history for eight centuries, come to be written on an island in the Atlantic?

Following the assassination of Austrian Archduke Franz Ferdinand in Sarajevo in 1914, the event that lit the blue touch paper of WWI, Karl became heir presumptive and when Emperor Franz Joseph died in November 1916, he succeeded to the Austrian throne. But by 1918 the Austrian empire was in tatters, new countries such as Czechoslovakia and Hungary being forged out of the ruins. With an Austrian Republic declared in 1919, Karl refused to abdicate or give up his claim to sovereignty and fled to Switzerland in March of that year.

After a couple of unsuccessful stabs at reclaiming the Hungarian throne, in November 1921 the British decided to exile Karl I and his wife to Madeira, a place from which it was thought he couldn't easily make another attempt. Originally billeted in the Villa Victoria near Reid's Palace Hotel, the family were later moved up to Monte and the Quinta do Monte. On a stroll into town, the unlucky Habsburg caught a cold that developed into pneumonia. He died on 1 April, 1922.

Beatified by Pope John Paul II in 2004, Karl's body lies in a simple flag-draped casket in a side chapel in Monte's Igreja da Nossa Senhora. Over the decades there has been talk of transferring the body to the Imperial Crypt in Vienna, but nothing has ever come of this. The chapel has become a shrine for royalists from across the former Habsburg empire who come to seek out this place where the Habsburg story came to its unlikely but definitive end.

trees and plunging gorges of Funchal is an unforgettable experience, often taking visitors above the low clouds that wreathe Madeira's mountain sides – but it's definitely not one for vertigo sufferers. The swaying cabins deliver visitors to Babosas, a short walk from Monte's sights. Nearby, another less-frequented cable car heads across to the botanical gardens.

Explore ◈
North Coast

Madeira's rugged north coast often feels a world away from the sun-splashed south, with high cliffs rising vertically from the seething Atlantic that pounds the island with full force. Three villages (Santana, São Vicente and Porto Moniz) have sufficient attractions for a day excursion from Funchal, but remember – while the south coast bathes in sunshine, the chilly north's damp air might mean it's time to fish the sweaters out.

The Short List

○ **Grutas e Centro do Vulcanismo (p91)** Exploring São Vicente's volcanic caves and the attached science centre.

○ **Aquário da Madeira (p92)** Meeting inhabitants of the Atlantic at this aquarium in an old fort.

○ **Piscinas Naturais (p91)** Taking the plunge at Porto Moniz' famous rock pools.

○ **Cachelote (p94)** Dining amid the volcanic rock pools of Porto Moniz.

○ **Quinta do Furão (p93)** Eating in Madeiran style at the north's best restaurant.

Getting There & Around
🚌 The north coast is served by two Funchal bus companies – Rodoeste and Horários do Funchal.

North Coast Map on p90

Porto Moniz YOLA WATRUCKA/GETTY IMAGES ©

For reviews see
- Experiences p91
- Eating p93

ATLANTIC OCEAN

10 km
5 miles

Piscinas Naturais
Centro Ciência Viva
Aquário da Madeira
Porto Moniz
Ribeira da Janela
North Coast Road
Seixal Beach
Seixal
São Vicente
Grutas e Centro do Vulcanismo
Ponta Delgada
Igreja do Bom Jesus
Thatched A-Frame Cottages
Parque Temático da Madeira
Santana
Faial
Porto da Cruz
Queimadas Forest Park
Pico Ruivo (1862m)
Pico do Arieiro (1818m)
Ribeiro Frio
Encumeada Pass
Serra de Água

ER101
ER104
ER110
VE2

Experiences

Grutas e Centro do Vulcanismo
CAVE

1 ◉ MAP P90, C3

Top billing on Madeira's north coast goes to this two-for-one attraction south of São Vicente. The first part of the experience is a guided tour of the local caves – 900,000-year-old lava tubes studied by English geologist James Johnson in the 1850s. The second part is the Centro do Vulcanismo – a 3D, interactive look at Madeira's volcanic birth and volcanoes in general. It's a real hit with the kids and a great wet-weather activity. (☏291 842 404; www.grutasecentrodovulcanismosaovicente.com; Sitio do pé do Passo, São Vicente; adult/child €8/6; ⏱10am-6pm; 🚻)

Piscinas Naturais
SWIMMING

2 ◉ MAP P90, A1

Natural pools made of volcanic rock (assisted by a dab of concrete here and there) can be found at both ends of Porto Moniz seafront. Those near the Cachalote restaurant are free and wild. Those at the other end charge admission, are a touch tamer and are better for swimming. (Rua dos Emigrantes & Rua do Forte de São João Baptista, Porto Moniz; admission €1.50; ⏱9am-5.30pm)

Porta da Cruz
VILLAGE

3 ◉ MAP P90, F3

The furthest point heading eastwards you can reach on the north coast before mammoth cliffs persuade the road to head inland, Porta da Cruz is a picturesque

Cave tour by Grutas d Centro do Vulcanismo

IRENA IRIS SZEWCZYK/SHUTTERSTOCK ©

spot nestling at the base of some seriously steep terraced slopes. One of Madeira's last working sugar mills fills the village with a sweet scent.

Seixal Beach BEACH

4 ⊙ MAP P90, B2

Seixal's black-sand beach can be accessed through an arch in the rock. It receives fewer visitors than beaches on the south coast, but check the weather forecast before heading here. (Seixal)

Igreja do Bom Jesus CHURCH

5 ⊙ MAP P90, D2

The fishing village of Ponta Delgada, 30km west of Santana, is worth a brief halt for its authentic remoteness and to visit the

A-frame cottage, Santana

TANE MAHUTA/GETTY IMAGES ©

baroque Igreja do Bom Jesus. The church houses an 18th-century crucifix that was mysteriously washed ashore in 1740. It also serves as the focus of the local Festa de Senhor Jesus, a few days in September when Ponta Delgada awakens from its slumber. (Ponta Delgada)

Aquário da Madeira AQUARIUM

6 ⊙ MAP P90, A1

Madeira's top aquarium hides away like a hermit crab in a renovated stone fortress. Inside, 12 tanks represent various ocean habitats around Madeira, the largest contains 500,000L of water and is big enough to accommodate divers. The whole colourful underwater world is here, though most visitors' attention is taken by the sharks in the big tank. (✆291 850 340; Rua Forte São João Batista, Porto Moniz; adult/child €7/4; ⏱10am-6pm; 👫)

North Coast Road LANDMARK

7 ⊙ MAP P90, A2

Road number 101 once struck fear into the heart of every Madeiran driver until it was retired to Room 101 by the modern VE2. The old route was the island's most dramatic and scenic road, the barely car-wide strip of tarmac clinging to the side of cliffs and splashed by waterfalls and waves. Some sections (one-way towards Porto Moniz) are still open. (Seixal to Porto Moniz)

Thatched A-Frame Cottages ARCHITECTURE

8 ◉ MAP P90, E3

This group of A-framed cottages stands in the centre of Santana and houses the tourist office, among other things. More authentic examples in various states of disrepair can be found in gardens dotted around Santana. (Sítio do Serrado, Santana; admission free; ⏱approximately 10am-6pm)

Parque Temático da Madeira AMUSEMENT PARK

9 ◉ MAP P90, E3

An engaging place to take the kids, this Madeira-themed park has a boating lake, a maze, a Monte train, mock-ups of Santana A-Frame houses, a large kiddies playground, along with some Madeira-specific exhibitions and a cafe. It's all quite informative but probably not worth a special trip from Funchal. (www.parquetematicodamadeira.pt; Estrada Regional 101, Santana; adult/child €6/4; ⏱10am-7pm; 👪)

Centro Ciência Viva MUSEUM

10 ◉ MAP P90, A1

This now-ageing centre covers a wide range of scientific topics in a hands-on way. The focus is on Madeira's Unesco-listed laurisilva forests, their climate, biodiversity and the human relationship with it. Interactive exhibits include a barefoot forest-floor walk, a virtual levada and heaps of touchscreens, puzzles and films. Sadly the

Northern Nights

Only Santana, São Vicente and Porto Moniz have any semblance of nightlife. People stay on the north coast for the very reason that there is only peace and quiet to enjoy after dark.

project has withered on the vine in recent years. (Rotunda do Ilhéu Mole, Porto Moniz; adult/child €3.50/2.50; ⏱10am-6pm; 👪)

Eating

Quinta do Furão INTERNATIONAL $$

11 ✗ MAP P90, E2

Stylishly rustic, this excellent hotel-restaurant sets the highest standards on the north coast. Wonderfully imaginative gourmet dishes, such as cream of beetroot soup with glazed chestnuts, foie gras infused with Madeira wine and quail marinated in sugar-cane molasses, blend international familiarity with a touch of exotic Macaronesia. Meals are taken indoors or out on the terrace with astonishing north-coast views.

Quinta do Furão is 3.8km north of Santana village centre – you'll need your own transport or a taxi to get there. (www.quintadofurao.com; Estrada Quinta do Furão 6, Santana; mains €9-20; ⏱noon-3.30pm & 6-9.30pm; 🛜)

Cantinho da Serra   MADEIRAN $$

12 🍴 MAP P90, E3

Located a five-minute drive from Santana heading towards Achada do Teixeira, this rustic inn creates a cosy atmosphere with its real log fires, hearty traditional Madeiran food and country decor. Meals are served in clay pots keeping the *bacalhau* (dried salt-cod), lamb and goat piping hot. The wines are mostly mainland affairs. (📞291 573 727; Estrada do Pico das Pedras, Santana; mains €9-17; ⏱noon-10pm)

Cachalote   MADEIRAN $$

13 🍴 MAP P90, A1

Around since the late 1960s, the 'Whale' wins the prize for Madeira's craziest restaurant location, sitting atop the crumbly volcanic rock on Port Moniz seafront, occasionally taking a wave from the furious Atlantic. Inside you'll discover an exhibition on the town's whaling and agricultural past before you reach the dining room and plates of limpets and scabbardfish with banana. (📞291 853 180; www.restau-rantecachalote.com; Rua Forte de São João Batista, Porto Moniz; mains €9-17; ⏱noon-11pm)

Restaurante Grutas   MADEIRAN $$

14 🍴 MAP P90, F3

Madeira's only cave-based eatery is this snack bar-restaurant en route from Faial to points south, selling Madeiran and international food. It's a fun stop after a day in the mountains and an unusual venue for a day-ending dinner. (📞291 572 817; Lombo de Baixo, Sítio da Degolada, Faial; mains €5-15; ⏱8.30am-10pm Mon-Sat; 📶)

Ferro Velho   MADEIRAN $

15 🍴 MAP P90, C3

A long-standing pub-restaurant in the cobbled streets of old São Vicente, this is the best place to cradle a Coral in the evenings if you're not driving back to the capital. Bedecked with football scarves and number plates from around the world, its food is cheap, but it's best to stick to the typically Madeiran menu items. (Rua da Fonte Velha, São Vicente; mains €3-9; ⏱11am-11pm; 📶)

Churrascaria Santana   PORTUGUESE $

Gourmets will shun this smoky local grill, but this is a superb spot (see 17 🍴 MAP P90, F3) to meet day-tripping families, forestry workers and Santana's police officers over slabs of cheap grilled meat and Portuguese reds. Tables are nicely laid with chequered tablecloths and the welcome is friendly. (Avenida Manuel Marques Trinidade, Santana; mains €8-12; ⏱10am-10pm)

Quebra Mar   MADEIRAN $$

16 🍴 MAP P90, C3

Located on São Vicente seafront, this outstanding restaurant serves up 360-degree views of the coast and seascape (the dining room actually revolves slowly), as well as meat and fish in equal measure. The focus is firmly on Madeiran

Cachalote

mainstays, such as scabbardfish, *espetada* (grilled beef skewers), tuna and fish stew. For dessert, go for the *pudim de veludo* (custard and caramel pudding). (☏ 291 842 338; www.restaurantequebramar.com; Sítio do Calhau, São Vicente; mains €8-16; ⌚9am-6pm Mon, to 10pm Tue-Sun)

Estrela do Norte   MADEIRAN $$

 MAP P90, F3

The 'Northern Star' seats 145 at formally laid, tightly packed tables, onto which waitresses plonk the

mainstays of Madeiran cuisine such as *espada* (scabbardfish) with banana, *espetada* (grilled beef skewers) and marinated pork. If you've had your fill of regional cuisine, there are also decent pizzas and house specials.

The cosy bar is the place to while away a chilling northern night if lingering longer. (Avenida Manuel Marques Trinidade 24, Santana; mains €7-14; ⌚10am-10pm)

Explore ⊛
East Madeira

Outside Funchal, East Madeira is the island's most heavily populated area. The 'second city' and former capital Machico, Madeira's main port at Caniçal, and the stilt-walking airport are all at this end of the island. It's an action-packed area of gliding Boeings and aqua parks, golden sand and stupendous views, all just a short ride from Funchal along the Via Rápida.

The Short List

○ **Camacha Wicker Factory (p98)** *Watching the basket weavers creating Madeira's traditional wickerware.*

○ **Museu da Baleia (p103)** *Visiting the best museum in the world dedicated to the whale and whaling.*

○ **Praia de Machico (p104)** *Working up a tan on Machico's manmade beach.*

○ **Prainha (p103)** *Taking it easy on East Madeira's idyllic black-sand beach.*

○ **Ponta de São Lourenço (p100)** *Hiking Madeira's sun-drenched eastern peninsula.*

Getting There & Around

🚌 SAM service 113 links Funchal with Caniço, Santa Cruz, the airport, Machico, Caniçal and Baía d'Abra. The airport is also connected to Funchal city centre and the Hotel Zone by a dedicated airport bus.

East Madeira Map on p102

Ponta de São Lourenço trail (p100) MAYA KARKALICHEVA/GETTY IMAGES ©

Top Experience 📷
Camacha Wicker Factory

Camacha is all about one traditional product – wicker. Harvested in the nearby mountains, it's dried and graded before being twisted and weaved into myriad objects of varying degrees of usefulness. The industry's epicentre is a building in the town centre called O Relógio (The Clock), which houses a workshop, shop and displays.

◎ MAP P102, B3

📞 291 922 777

Largo Conselheiro Aires de Ornelas 12, Camacha

admission free

⏱ 8.45am-6pm

Basket Cases

This being Madeira (an island of steep hills), the O Relógio building is entered on the 2nd floor, where you'll find the shop. Half exhibition, half souvenir emporium, its wicker comes in all shapes and sizes, from huge mirror frames and doll's house furniture to suitcases, mini Monte toboggans and wine bottle holders. Prices are very reasonable and the quality extremely high – items often last for decades.

Weird & Wonderful World of Wicker

Down a level from the shop, an exhibition of wicker creations will have you reaching for your camera. A wicker replica of caravel sails like those used by Zarco (the explorer who claimed the islands for Portugal) towards the stairs, while wicker monkeys and frogs stare back at you with old-fashioned teddy-bear eyes. You won't be reaching for your wallet here, though – no matter how much you offer, sadly none of this is for sale. What is for sale are the large pieces of furniture, very popular among Madeira's smaller guesthouses and *quinta* (estate) hotels.

Fabrica

Arguably the most interesting part of O Relógio is the basement where four or five nimble-fingered local craftspeople sit on old cushions creating items for the shop. They'll gladly demonstrate their skill and let you handle the items they make, but few speak any English. Here you can also see the crude wooden templates they use to fashion baskets and lampshades, as well as inspect the bushels of graded wicker stacked up against the walls.

★ Top Tips

o The town is 700m above sea level, meaning the weather is invariably cooler here than in Funchal. Many are caught out by this.

o The shop can ship furniture to your home address, but nothing smaller.

o The viewing terrace behind O Relógio has amazing views 700m down to the Atlantic.

o Kids will enjoy the large playground on the square in front of O Relógio.

✕ Take a Break

The Madeiran restaurant in O Relógio (p106), above the wicker shop and factory, is the best option for a full meal. The cafe next to the shop has cakes, coffees and sandwiches.

Walking Tour 🚶

Ponta de São Lourenço

This there-and-back coastal walk takes hikers to the far eastern end of Madeira, the Ponta de São Lourenço peninsula. The trail along the island's snaking, undulating tail is a very different beast to the famous levada walks, with lots of ups and downs and no shade. A lack of vegetation means nothing gets in the way of the Atlantic panoramas, which at some points will leave you breathless.

Walk Facts

Start & Finish Baía D'Abra car park

Length 8km, four hours

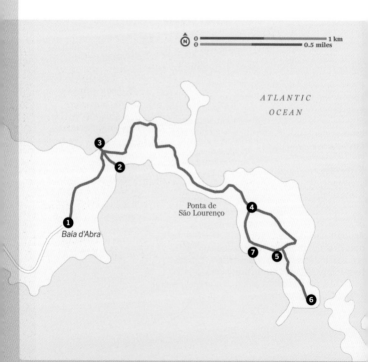

❶ Baía D'Abra

Buses and taxis leave hikers at the Baía D'Abra car park, where you'll find a route map (numbered PR8) but little else. There are occasionally refreshments here but they tend to appear in the second half of the day.

❷ Take a Dip

Around 15 to 20 minutes into the hike you reach a crossroads in the trail. Take a right and follow the rough path down to a very secluded beach that's good for a dip in the sea. In the morning you'll have this and the views of the Desertas to yourself.

❸ Seahorse Rocks

Head up from the beach and keep going straight on. This dead end has camera-friendly views of the seahorse rocks, toweringly stranded chunks of volcanic rock that the seething Atlantic has separated from the mothership. The reds and greys of the rocks contrast photogenically with the white surf.

❹ Left or Right

An information board giving details of the protected area you are passing through stands at the beginning/end of the loop around the end of the accessible part of the peninsula. It doesn't matter which way you go, as you'll end up back here. We're going left.

❺ Cais do Sardinha

Built by Manuel Bettencourt Sardinha in 1905 as a holiday home, Cais do Sardinha is a pretty, tropical oasis of a house that was sold to the regional government by his granddaughter in 1996. It now serves as a reception centre for the protected area. Picnic tables here provide the perfect lunch spot.

❻ Morro do Furado

Behind the Cais do Sardinha rises the Morro do Furado, a huge hillside marking the end of the peninsula's accessible section. It's a bit of a slog to the top on crumbly and slippery ground, but the Atlantic panoramas from the top are magnificent.

❼ Quay & Beach

Looping back, just past the bird-watching post, a short path runs down to a small quay and beach, a secluded spot even when the trail is busy. Swimming and diving are permitted. From here retrace your steps back to Baía D'Abra.

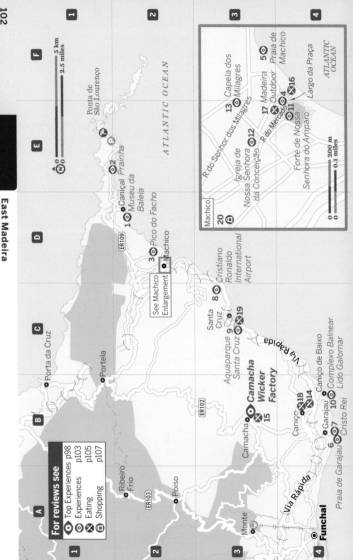

East Madeira

For reviews see
● Top Experiences p98
● Experiences p103
✕ Eating p105
🅐 Shopping p107

ATLANTIC OCEAN

Ponta de
São Lourenço

Canical ● 1
Prainha
Museu da ● 2
Baleia
Pico do Facho ● 3
Machico ●

See Machico
Enlargement

Cristiano ● 8
Ronaldo
International
Airport

Santa
Cruz
Aquaparque ● 9 ✕ 19
Santa Cruz

Camacha Wicker
Factory

Porta da Cruz ●

Portela ●

Ribeiro
Frio ●

Poiso ●

Camacha ●
✕ 15

Canico ●
✕ 18
✕ 14

Caniço de Baixo
Garajau ● ● 10 Complexo Balnear
6 ● ● 7 Lido Galomar
Cristo Rei ●

Praia de Garajau ●

Via Rápida

Monte ●

Funchal ●

ATLANTIC OCEAN

Machico

Igreja de
Nossa Senhora
da Conceição ● 12

R. do Senhor dos Milagres

Capela dos
Milagres ● 13

Madeira ● 17
Outdoor ✕ 16
R. do Mercado
Nossa Senhora ● 11
Forte de Nossa
Senhora do Amparo

Praia de ● 5
Machico

● 4

Largo da Praça

ATLANTIC
OCEAN

🅐 20

N
0 ——— 5 km
0 ——— 2.5 miles

0 ——— 200 m
0 ——— 0.1 miles

ER109
ER102
ER103

Experiences

Museu da Baleia MUSEUM

1 MAP P102, D2

Once a minor exhibition housed in small seafront building, Caniçal's Whale Museum was moved to a large multi-million-euro, ultra-modern complex in 2012, making it possibly the world's best museum devoted to the topic. The fascinating exhibition is divided into two sections – whaling on Madeira and whales – with an automatic commentary playing in your ears as you go. Count on spending at least 2½ hours here. (www.museudabaleia.org; Rua Garcia Moniz 1, Caniçal; adult/child incl audioguide €10/5; 10.30am-6pm Tue-Sun)

Prainha BEACH

2 MAP P102, E1

For those in the know, this tiny beach east of Caniçal is the best outside Funchal. A romantically secluded suntrap, this wild arc of black sand is backed by cliffs under which there's a basic cafe. At high tide the water comes right up to the rocks leaving no sand – get there early and you'll have the place to yourself (for a while at least). There's parking on the clifftop and Caniçal buses stop here on request. (ER214)

Pico do Facho VIEWPOINT

3 MAP P102, D2

When you get bored of lying on Machico beach, the climb up to Pico do Facho that rises above the

Museu da Baleia

town to the north is a great way to spend an afternoon. By car, take the ER109 towards the old tunnel heading towards Caniçal. Turn right just before the tunnel and climb until you reach the top. The views of Machico, the airport and out across the endless Atlantic are simply stupendous.

There's also a year-round refreshments stand, a barbecue area and lots of cats to keep you company up there. (Machico)

Madeira Outdoor   OUTDOORS

4 ⊙ MAP P102, E4

Excellent tour company based in Machico specialising in every kind of outdoor activity you could imagine, from birdwatching and levada walks to coasteering and surfing. It is one of the best agencies to contact for canyoning in Madeira's mountains. (📞966 230 212; www.madeiraoutdoor.com; shop 7, Praça do Mercado Municipal, Machico; canyoning tours €60-180, levada walks from €36)

Praia de Machico   BEACH

5 ⊙ MAP P102, F3

Madeira's best artificial beach is this gently sloping suntrap created with golden sand shipped in from Morocco and protected by two artificial breaks. Facilities include toilets, a volleyball court and showers. There are a couple of places to eat nearby as you watch planes gliding low across the mouth of the bay. (Rua do Leiria, Machico)

Praia de Garajau   BEACH

6 ⊙ MAP P102, B4

At the foot of the cliff atop which stands the Cristo Rei statue, this stony beach was once used for dismembering and boiling up whales caught by boats off Madeira. It's since been turned into a leisure complex with a restaurant and other facilities, reached by cable car near the statue or a very long and zigzagging road. (Estrada do Cristo Rei, Garajau; cable car single/return €2/2.50)

Cristo Rei   STATUE

7 ⊙ MAP P102, B4

The upmarket village of Garajau hangs for dear life on the side of a cliff, 6km as the crow flies from central Funchal. On an often blustery promontory below the village stands the *Cristo Rei* – a late-1920s mini-version of Rio's *Christ the Redeemer* statue, arms outspread, eyes gazing into the infinite blue of the Atlantic. (Estrada Nova de Cristo Rei, Garajau)

Cristiano Ronaldo International Airport   LANDMARK

8 ⊙ MAP P102, C3

Few airports could be counted as true places of interest, but Madeira's runway sticking out on stilts into the Atlantic and hemmed on two sides by mountains definitely can be. From Santa Cruz head uphill along the ER207 that runs high above the runway for great views of planes performing the tricky landing manoeuvre. You can also plane watch from the airport's roof as you wait for your flight. (www.ana.pt; Santa Cruz)

Aquaparque Santa Cruz
WATER PARK

9 ◉ MAP P102, C3

Madeira's only water park is a quite modest affair situated in a ravine to the southwest of Santa Cruz. Despite the posted opening hours, it only really operates in the hottest of the summer months (July and August). (www.aquaparquemadeira.com; Ribeira da Boaventura, Santa Cruz; adult/child €9/6, after 2pm €7/5; ☺10am-6pm Jun-Jul & Sep-Nov, to 7pm Aug)

Complexo Balnear Lido Galomar
BEACH

10 ◉ MAP P102, B4

Take the lift down from Caniço de Baixo's Hotel Galomar to discover this secluded sun-trapping bathing area with sea access, pools and a first-rate restaurant. (☎291 930 930; www.galoresort.com; Ponta da Oliveira, Caniço de Baixo; admission free; ☺8am-midnight)

Forte de Nossa Senhora do Amparo
FORTRESS

11 ◉ MAP P102, E4

The triangular, ochre fortress on the Machico seafront dates from 1706 and was built to protect the town from pirates. There's not much to see here save for a few old cannons. It once served as the tourist office

but is now home to the local MEP's surgery. (Machico seafront)

Igreja de Nossa Senhora da Conceição
CHURCH

12 ◉ MAP P102, E3

The main church in Machico is one of the island's largest, reflecting the town's erstwhile status as Madeira's capital. The musty, ancient-feeling interior is adorned with a baroque inventory but strangely no *azulejos* (hand-painted tiles). (Largo Dr Antonio Jardim D'Oliveira, Machico)

Capela dos Milagres
CHAPEL

13 ◉ MAP P102, E3

Machico has three churches but the most famous is the pretty little Miracles Chapel on the north side of the river. It was famously washed away in a flood in 1803, but the crucifix was found bobbing in the Atlantic by an American galley. 'Miracle!' the locals declared, hence the chapel's name. (Rua do Senhor dos Milagres, Machico)

Eating

La Perla
INTERNATIONAL $$$

14 ✖ MAP P102, B4

Occupying the original 19th-century mansion house at the Quinta Splendida, this gourmet restaurant serves the most exquisite meals on this stretch of the coast. Take a seat in one of the three rooms to enjoy a seasonal menu, with the flambéed dishes a speciality of the house. For

The Machin Legend

Some claim Machico is named after Robert Machin, a 14th-century Bristol merchant who was washed up here while eloping with his lover, Anne of Hertford. The 'discoverer' of Madeira, Captain Zarco, is supposed to have stumbled across their graves when first stepping ashore.

dessert, go for the crêpe Suzette, flambéed with Grand Marnier and orange sauce. (www.quintasplendida.com; Estrada da Ponta Oliveira 11, Caniço; menu €60, mains €15-30; 7-10pm Wed, Fri & Sun)

Atlantis
MADEIRAN $$

The aptly named Atlantis (see 10 Map p102, B4) looks as though it's risen from the waves and clamped itself to the cliffside above the suntrap beach below the Galomar Hotel. Seating options are on chunky wicker inside, or out on the terrace above the crashing Atlantic. You'd expect an exclusively seafood menu, but meat and even uncommon dishes like duck make an appearance. (291 930 930; Ponta D'Oliveira, Caniço de Baixo; mains €11.50-15; 10am-10pm; 🛜)

O Relógio
MADEIRAN $$

15 ⊗ MAP P102, B3

O Relógio, above the Camacha wicker shop and factory, is the best eating option in town for a full meal. It has many Madeiran staples on the menu and the views from the dining room are stupendous. (Largo Conselieiro Aires de Ornelas, Camacha; mains €8-14.50; noon-4pm Nov-Mar, noon-4pm & 7-10pm Apr-Oct)

Maré Alta
SEAFOOD $$

16 ⊗ MAP P102, F4

This seafront glass box, just metres from the waves, contains Machico's best seafood restaurant. Every inhabitant of Madeira's waters, plus many from elsewhere, swims in shoals through the menu, which includes local limpets, tuna, *espada* (scabbardfish), octopus and imported shellfish. (Largo da Praça, Machico; mains €10-18; 11am-11pm)

Mercado Velho
MADEIRAN $$

17 ⊗ MAP P102, E3

Ensconced in the former market building, this long-established restaurant just back from the seafront has a pretty outdoor seating area gathered around the old market sinks, as well as a more formal indoor space. The eclectic menu includes meat and fish, as well as pastas, soups and salads. (Rua do Mercado, Machico; mains €10-18.50; 10am-11pm)

A Central
PORTUGUESE, BRAZILIAN $$

18 ⊗ MAP P102, B4

A smoky aroma of grilling meat wafts from the door of this central Caniço *churrascaria* (traditional

Cristo Rei (p104)

grill). Meat and fish, expertly barbecued on acacia cinders and served with salad and wine, is the deal here. The *rodizio brasileiro* – 14 types of skewered meat – sorts the carnivores from the kids. (Rua João Paulo II 10-14, Caniço; mains €8-15; ⏰11am-2am)

Boca de Panela   SEAFOOD $$

19 ✖ MAP P102, C3

Arguably Santa Cruz's best place to dine, this mid-naughties block near the aquapark has floor-to-ceiling plate-glass windows providing ocean views and an opportunity to watch the planes gliding past the windows on their approach to the nearby airport. The menu is a mix of Madeiran and imported seafood, the service polite. (☎291 600 267; seafront near Aquapark, Santa Cruz; mains €10-20; ⏰10am-midnight Tue-Sun)

Shopping

Casa das Bordadeiras de Machico   ARTS & CRAFTS

20 🏢 MAP P102, D3

This tiny (work)shop belonging to a local cooperative is the place to pick up some authentic, locally made embroidery. Keeps slightly erratic hours and staff speak no English. It's a 10-minute walk southwest from the bus station. (☎291 966 655; Pontinha, ER101; ⏰9am-6pm Mon-Fri)

Driving Tour 🎡

Driving through Eastern Madeira

This rollercoaster drive around Madeira's eastern half takes in dramatic mountain vistas, sleepy coastal villages and some fine spots to sample local fare, from mountain trout to coastal limpets. Do it in your own hire car, so you can spend as much time as you like at each stop.

Route Facts
Start Monte
Finish Caniço de Baixo
Length 86km, five hours

❶ Monte

You might have already seen Monte's attractions, but a second visit can be a completely different experience. At 500m above sea level, Madeira's fickle weather can change dramatically up here, wreathing the Igreja da Nossa Senhora (p85) in dense fog or bathing it in sunshine.

❷ Casa de Abrigo do Poiso

From Monte, the almost vertical drive north takes you to Poiso, where the cosy inn Casa de Abrigo do Poiso (p137) stands at the turn-off for Pico do Arieiro. It's a nice spot for a mid-morning snack.

❸ Pico do Arieiro

The drive to the top of Pico do Arieiro takes you well above the tree line and ends at the radar station, cafe, souvenir shop and very steep car park that crowd around the summit. On a clear day, the views from here are simply stupendous.

❹ Ribeiro Frio

The only way from Pico do Arieiro is down, back to Poiso, from where it's around 15 minutes of up-down driving to the nippy village of Ribeiro Frio. Restaurants here serve local trout, which can be seen chasing each other in endless circles at the **trout farm** (p136).

❺ Faial

Cowering picturesquely under the Penha D'Águia (Eagle's Rock), a massive hulk of rock rising almost 600 vertical metres from the Atlantic, the north-coast village of Faial is a sleepy, undervisited place with a pretty church and a couple of cafes.

❻ Machico

Take the fast road through several tunnels to lively Machico, Madeira's second 'city', former capital and the spot where explorer Zarco first stepped ashore to claim Madeira for Portugal. The town has several undemanding sights, an artificial beach and some good restaurants.

❼ Santa Cruz

As the village at the end of Madeira airport's runway, the most memorable thing about Santa Cruz might be the sight of planes gliding low over the rocky beach as they attempt to hit the tarmac.

❽ Caniço

Now virtually attached to Funchal by urban sprawl, Caniço has a tiny historical centre boasting an attractive church and the Quinta Splendida gardens. Head downhill to quieter Caniço de Baixo to watch the sunset from the suntrap bathing area of Complexo Balnear Lido Galomar (p105).

Explore

West Madeira

West of Funchal is where the Madeiran sun shines brightest, with long light-filled days, dramatic sunsets, and millions of the island's sweet miniature bananas and Malvasia grapes ripening in the heat. Varied and scenically dramatic, there's a lot to see and do off the slow road west, from the fishing traditions of Câmara de Lobos to the cutting-edge art of Calheta.

The Short List

○ **Cabo Girão (p113)** *Going weak at the knees on the glass platform hanging over this 580m-high sea cliff.*

○ **Museu Etnográfico da Madeira (p113)** *Getting the lowdown on Madeira's traditional culture.*

○ **Paúl do Mar (p113)** *Wandering the pretty lanes of this western surfing village.*

○ **Mudas Museu (p114)** *Appreciating the contemporary installations at Calheta's top attraction.*

Getting There & Around

🚌 Rodoeste (www.rodoeste.com.pt) has a monopoly on bus transport west of Funchal. While almost all west-heading coaches serve Câmara de Lobos, other communities have only a skeleton service with just a couple of buses a day.

West Madeira Map on p112

Câmara de Lobos (p115) PAWEL KAZMIERCZAK/SHUTTERSTOCK ©

West Madeira

For reviews see

Experiences	p113
Eating	p115
Drinking	p117
Shopping	p117

0   5 km
0   2.5 miles

N

Ponta do Pargo

Ponta do Pargo ● 8

ER101

ER110

ER23

Paúl do Mar ● 2

ER110

Calheta

13 ●
4 ● 11 ●
● 6

Mudas Museu
Engenhos da Calheta
Praia da Calheta

● 10

Madalena
do Mar

Ponta do Sol ● 7

Ribeira Brava ●
See Ribeira Brava
Enlargement

ATLANTIC
OCEAN

VE1

São Vicente

ER104

Central Valley

Paúl da
Serra

Encumeada
Pass

Serra de Água

VE4

Central Valley

ER107

Curral das
Freiras

Jardim da
Serra

16 ●

Henriques &
Henriques

Cabo Girão

Câmara de Lobos

Funchal ●

5 ●

15 14 12

Ribeira Brava

Museu Etnográfico
da Madeira

20 ●

17 ●
18 ●

9 ●

Igreja de
São Bento

● 3

● 19

0   200 m
0   0.1 miles

Experiences

Cabo Girão VIEWPOINT

1 ⊙ MAP P112, E4

Around 3km west of Câmara de Lobos, Madeira's highest sea cliffs – whose name means means 'Cape of Return' – rise 580m to loom high over the village and the Atlantic's sapphire expanse. The panorama from the viewing platform is nothing short of spectacular. Spectacular that is, unless you look down – the platform floor is made of glass and hangs over the cliff edge – a knee-weakening, toe-curling experience! Many Rodoeste services heading west now climb up here from Funchal. (⊙24hr)

Paúl do Mar VILLAGE

2 ⊙ MAP P112, B2

Perching precariously on a ledge under high cliffs, pretty Paúl do Mar is the surfing capital of the Atlantic and has even hosted a leg of the World Surfing Championships. Its narrow lanes are a joy to explore, with their pretty cottages and flower pots. Rodoeste buses 80, 142 and a couple of obscure services make the run here from Funchal. (ER223)

Museu Etnográfico da Madeira MUSEUM

3 ⊙ MAP P112, B3

One of Madeira's most interesting museums, the collections here look at every aspect of the island's traditional life, from *espada*

Paúl do Mar

(scabbardfish) fishing to wicker weaving, wine production to toboggan transport. There's an old shop complete with till nostalgically still taking *escudos* (Portugal's currency before the euro), live weaving demonstrations and fascinating temporary exhibitions to inspect. (Rua de São Francisco 24, Ribeira Brava; adult/concession €3/1.50; ⏲9.30am-5pm Tue-Fri, 10am-12.30pm & 1.30-5.30pm Sat)

Mudas Museu — MUSEUM

4 ◉ MAP P112, B3

Housed in an almost Minecraft-like building high above Calheta, this contemporary arts space has a gallery, shop, cafe, auditorium and workshop area. The exhibitions here change every two months or so and Paulo David's dramatic architectural achievement in basalt is admirable. It's worth getting a taxi from the beach as it's a hard slog on foot. (☏291 820 900; Estrada Simão Gonçalves da Câmara 37, Calheta; admission €4; ⏲10am-5pm Tue-Sun)

Henriques & Henriques — WINERY

5 ◉ MAP P112, E4

Widely regarded by those in the know as the island's best wine producer, Henriques & Henriques only uses grapes from its own vineyards in Quinta Grande and Câmara de Lobos. The wine is finished off in huge barrels at its modern, specially designed headquarters. Visitors can try the four types of three-year-old wine for free. Anything older normally incurs a charge. (www.henriquese henriques.pt; Avenida da Autonomia 10, Câmara de Lobos; admission free; ⏲9am-1pm & 2.30-5.30pm Mon-Fri)

Praia da Calheta — BEACH

6 ◉ MAP P112, B3

Two well-protected artificial beaches (created with sand from western Sahara) face each other off on Calheta's seafront, one of the sunniest places on the island. A great place to swim on hot days and there are plenty of eating spots and a supermarket nearby. (Rua Dom Manuel I, Calheta)

Ponta do Sol — VILLAGE

7 ◉ MAP P112, C3

This village is the island's sunniest spot (hence the name) and has a rocky beach and a pretty, compact centre. It's worth a stop on the way between Funchal and Calheta.

Ponta do Pargo — VIEWPOINT

8 ◉ MAP P112, A1

Madeira's most westerly point is Ponta do Pargo (Red Snapper Point). From the village of the same name, a 2km trail heads out to a lighthouse from where there are spectacular Atlantic vistas – an especially good spot to find yourself at sundown. (Ponta do Pargo; admission free)

Igreja de São Bento CHURCH

9 ⊙ MAP P112, A4

Originally dating from the 15th century, one of the most attractive churches on Madeira occupies a pebble square in the very centre of Ribeira Brava. Almost as wide as it is long, the three-nave interior is divided by high Gothic arches, which reach up to a curved, embossed ceiling. From this hang the church's most impressive feature: two giant crystal chandeliers. There are Manueline elements throughout, such as the carved stone font and the pulpit. (www.igrejarbrava.com; Rua dos Camachos, Ribeira Brava; ⏰8am-6pm Mon-Sat, from 7am Sun)

Madalena do Mar VILLAGE

10 ⊙ MAP P112, C3

Wedged into the mouth of an impossibly deep creek, tiny Madalena do Mar has a long stony beach and a quiet, undisturbed atmosphere that feels a long way from Funchal. (ER101)

Engenhos da Calheta MUSEUM

11 ⊙ MAP P112, B3

Calheta's old sugar refinery building starts as a half-hearted 'museum' and ends as a shop where you can buy the *bolo de mel* (molasses cake), molasses, rum and *poncha* (local sugar-cane spirit drink) still made somewhere on the premises. (Calheta Sugar Refinery; ☎291 822 264; www.facebook.com/sociedadedosengenhosdacalheta/;

The Fishers of Câmara de Lobos

Madeira's signature fish is the long, eel-like *espada* (scabbard-fish), which is caught at night by the fisherfolk from Câmara de Lobos. These hardy souls can be seen knocking back dangerous amounts of *poncha* (local sugar-cane spirit drink) in the village's many small bars before heading to the tiny Capela de Nossa Senhora da Conceição to ask for a safe night at sea. The catch is brought in early next morning and sold off to the island's markets and restaurants, after which the fisherfolk of Câmara de Lobos return to the bars to celebrate another battle with the fickle Atlantic won.

Avenida D Manuel I 29, Calheta; admission free; ⏰8am-7pm Mon-Fri, from 10am Sat & Sun)

Eating

Ilhéu MADEIRAN $$

12 ✖ MAP P112, E4

All bare walls, exposed lightbulbs and stylised *azulejos* (hand-painted tiles), the most recent addition to the Câmara de Lobos dining scene is this stylish little bistro, opened by the Madeiran president himself. Watch your Madeiran fish and meat dishes being prepared in the open kitchen before relaxing with a local wine. (☎961 878 202; Rua São João de

Deus 6, Câmara de Lobos; mains €10-15.50; ⏰11am-6pm Mon, to midnight Tue-Thu, 11am-3pm & 6pm-1am Fri & Sat, 11am-4pm Sun; 🛜)

Convento das Vinhas
MADEIRAN, INTERNATIONAL $$

13 🍴 MAP P112, B2

Perched high above Calheta, this family-run place, not far from the Mudas Museu, serves up excellent food with a hefty side of panoramic views. Madeiran and Portuguese favourites pack the menu, but this is possibly the only place on Madeira where you can order a local delicacy – *ovas de espada* – scabbardfish eggs. (Caminho Lombo do Salão 35, Calheta; mains €8-14; ⏰11am-11pm Mon-Sat, to 10pm Sun)

Fish at Vila do Peixe

HOLGER LEUE/LOOK-FOTO/GETTY IMAGES ©

Vila do Peixe
SEAFOOD $$

14 🍴 MAP P112, E4

This contemporary place is Câmara de Lobos' best seafood restaurant, offering the highest quality Madeiran fare. The fish, including parrot fish, red bream, *dourada* (sea bream) and *espada* (scabbardfish) are sold by weight, lightly salted and grilled to perfection on acacia embers. Local seafood include limpets, whelks and occasionally octopus. There's sometimes live music in the evenings, including fado and Madeiran folk. (📞291 099 909; www.viladopeixe.com; Rua Dr João Abel de Freitas 30A, Câmara de Lobos; mains €8.50-16.50; ⏰noon-11pm)

Vila da Carne
PORTUGUESE $$

15 🍴 MAP P112, E4

The sister restaurant of Vila do Peixe is the 'House of Meat', a clean-cut eatery specialising in traditional *espetada* (chunks of beef covered in salt, garlic and laurel leaf, impaled on a green laurel skewer and grilled over acacia embers). Interesting sides include sweet potatoes with molasses and typical Madeiran *milho frito* (fried corn cubes). (Rua Dr João Abel Freitas 30, Câmara de Lobos; mains €6-16; ⏰noon-11pm)

Quinta da Serra
INTERNATIONAL $$

16 🍴 MAP P112, E3

The French chef at this luxury hotel restaurant in the settlement of Jardim da Serra (north of Câmara de Lobos) cooks up an imaginative, international menu using only organic ingredients – a first for Madeira. The dining room is an elegant affair kept toasty in winter with a log burner, and the service is impeccable. (291 640 120; www. hotelquintadaserra.com; Estrada do Chote 4/6, Jardim da Serra; mains €10-20; 1-3pm & 6.30-10pm)

Muralha
PORTUGUESE $$

17 MAP P112, A4

This crimson box and terrace set high above the bay is a relaxed place to end the day. The menu is a mixed bag of grilled meat and fish – the Madeiran dishes to go for are the grilled tuna steak and *espetada* (traditionally grilled beef skewers). Or try the roasted codfish with prawns and mussels, if you're feeling more in a mainland mood. (291 952 592; Estrada Regional 220 1, Ribeira Brava; mains €10-19; 11am-11pm Sun & Tue-Thu, to 2am Fri & Sat)

Borda D'Agua
PORTUGUESE $$

18 MAP P112, A4

Right on the seafront as the name suggests, this multitasking eatery can serve as a lunchtime quickie for coffee and sandwiches outside, or as a full-blown fresh-fish dinner venue in the more formal restaurant setting inside. Madeiran specialities co-habit with pizzas and sandwiches on the food menu, and *poncha* (local sugar-cane spirit drink) mixes with Portuguese reds on the drinks card. (291 957 697; Rua Pereira Ribeiro, Ribeira Brava; mains €7.50-18; 8am-11pm)

Drinking

O Herédia
CAFE

19 MAP P112, B3

Slightly away from the tourists, this tiny cafe spreads tables across sunny Largo dos Herédias near Ribeira Brava's Ethnographical Museum. Serves coffees, beers, spirits and light meals. (Largo dos Herédias, Ribeira Brava; 7am-midnight Mon-Sat, 8am-9pm Sun)

Shopping

Provecto
SHOES

20 MAP P112, A4

One of only three craftsmen left on the island who can make the traditional Madeiran *botachã* (leather ankle boots), Duarte Roche creates more modern handmade shoes based on their design. Give him two days and he can tailor-make a pair of shoes for just €70 – these can also be shipped back home for you. Wonderful souvenirs from a true artisan. (925 802 026; Estrada Regional 104, Ribeira Brava; 9am-7pm Mon-Fri, to noon Sat)

West Madeira Drinking

Top Experience 📷
Levada Paths

One of the reasons people come to Madeira is to hike the levadas – 2500km of irrigation channels along which gentle paths lead through the wilds. A levada walk is the quintessential Madeira experience. Depart Funchal early in the morning, wander the dramatic landscape, picnicking along the way, and make it back into the city for dinner. Try at least one – most visitors are hooked straightaway.

🚌 Levada walks are normally accessible by bus, though this is not always the case.

🚗 Many walkers arrange for a taxi to wait at the end of the route to return them to Funchal.

Going it Alone

There aren't many levada walks you can't tackle on your own. However, accessing the start of the trail can take some planning, especially if you don't have a hire car. All of Madeira's bus companies now post their timetables online and routes are designed with tourists and walkers in mind. The tourist office in Funchal can help out with planning, as can hotel receptions. Doing things by car creates a problem as levada walks are linear routes, meaning you might need a bus to get you back to where you parked. Taxis are a good solution but can make the day an expensive affair.

Joining a Group

Every day tens of groups leave for the levadas on half- and full-day hikes. While these take care of the logistics of getting to and from the walk, groups often move fast and you don't have the freedom to tarry where you like for as long as you like. Tours are cheap (around €25 for a full-day hike), guides usually very clued up and you are often picked up and dropped off at your accommodation by the tour company. However groups can be large, clogging up the narrow paths and scaring off wildlife. Cruise-ship groups can be particularly huge. Lunch is sometimes provided for an extra charge and bookings can be made at countless places throughout the Hotel Zone.

Maps & Guidebooks

If you are heading out alone, having a map and/or specialist guidebook is recommended. The Sunflower guides to Madeira by John and Pat Underwood set the standard and are widely available on the island (even at supermarkets in the Hotel Zone). *Levadas and Footpaths of Madeira* by Raimundo Quintal is a little out of date but gives a lot of background. Cicerone's *Walking in Madeira* maps out 60 routes across the island while *Walk Madeira* by Shirley and Mike Whitehead plots a range of hikes for all abilities. *Madeira Tour and Trail* 1:40,000, available on Madeira, is one of the best maps around.

★ Top Tips

o It's often a good idea to contact the tourist office to find out if the route you intend to take is affected by the weather or repair work.

o Good hiking boots, a torch, waterproofs and food are a must.

o Exposed sections are common and definitely not for vertigo sufferers.

o Never walk in the levadas, throw anything into them or (how should we put it?) use them as an outdoor convenience.

✕ Take a Break

Taking a break on the levadas is simple: pack a picnic. There are precious few eating options on the paths themselves.

Story of the Levadas

Many countries around the world have created irrigation systems but none are quite like Madeira's levadas. Apart from being a feat of engineering, determination and ingenuity, it's their accessibility and the truly spectacular landscapes to which they give access that make them truly unique. They are the lifeblood of the island, providing water to taps, fields and gardens, and electricity to homes and businesses through hydroelectric power. Madeira has no real stable rivers, so without them human habitation on the island would be nigh on impossible.

So how did this small island come to have such a mammoth network of levadas? The first settlers soon realised that the rainfall and mist that drenched the mountainous interior somehow needed to be channelled down to the warm, dry south coast. Over 2 metres of precipitation a year can fall in the north of the island while the fertile south coast may not see a drop for half a year. Work began in the 16th century on creating fast-flowing aqueducts and over the next three centuries the network was developed, often using slave labour. Many died carving out the channels through impossibly rugged mountainscapes but by the 1900s 1000km of levadas were supplying water for agriculture and for drinking.

But there was a problem – many levadas were privately owned and the distribution of precious water was often unfair. In 1939 the state stepped in to study the irrigation system and commission more channels. By 1970 the system was essentially complete, though minor work is still ongoing. The island's longest levadas such as the Levada do Norte and the Levada dos Tornos were built at this time and are vital pieces of infrastructure.

As you enjoy a leisurely levada stroll, spare a thought for those who maintain the hundreds of kilometres of channels, tunnels, bridges, reservoirs, ducts and sluices. Around 99% of the system can only be accessed on foot – tools and materials have to be hauled by teams of workers sometimes tens of kilometres to where a rock fall or a landslip has caused a snarl-up. You will often meet these hardy work gangs on the trails.

Ribeiro Frio to Portela

○ **Start** Restaurante Ribeiro Frio
○ **Finish** Portela
○ **Length** 11km, 4 hours

One of the best and most easily accessible levada walks on the island, this classic route runs from chilly Ribeiro Frio through some rip-roaringly spectacular landscapes, across the sides of sheer cliffs and through the thick Unesco-protected laurisilva forest ending at Portela, with the fast-flowing Levada do Furado accompanying you most of the way.

Horários do Funchal buses 56 and 103 drop you off at the Restaurante Ribeiro Frio (p137), behind which you will find the beginning of the

Hiker en route from Ribeiro Frio to Portela

Levada do Furado – the path is signposted PR10.

After an hour, the bridge where the Levada do Furado is joined by another levada is a good place to stop for lunch – the **Ribeira do Poço do Bezerro**. It's a lovely spot with the sound of gurgling water, rustling trees and birdsong all around.

After about 1¼ hours the path and levada pass through a huge **cleft in the rock**. From the outside it looks as though you might need a torch to pass through but this isn't the case. Follow the stepping stones until your reach the end.

Things get tight after around two hours when the levada and the path squeeze onto a ledge cut out of the escarpment called the **Cabeça Furado**. Some parts here are pretty exposed and you need to watch your footing.

After around 2¾ hours you should reach the **Lamaceiros forestry station** from where you should be able to see the Ponta de São Lourenço. From here it's all downhill with more spectacular views. The going is very easy from here.

The Levada do Furado ends at Lamaceiros and you now pick up the **Levada da Portela**, either a gurgling rush of water or a dry

concrete channel, depending on where water is needed. On the way down, it's not difficult to spot the massive Penha D'Águia (Eagle's Rock) and the village of Faial on the north coast.

The descent into **Portela** passes the reservoir that stores the levada's water for future distribution. When you reach the road at the end of the path, turn left for Portela. SAM buses 53 and 78 make the trip back to Funchal.

Levada do Caldeirão Verde

○ **Start & Finish** Queimadas

○ **Length** 13km, 4 hours

A popular levada, the PR9 route is one of the most picturesque on Madeira, running for 6.5km (plus 6.5km back) through show-stopping landscapes. The levada pushes through some impossible territory, clinging to the sides of vertical rock faces and burrowing through tunnels. A torch is essential for this hike, as might be swimwear for a dip at the end.

To reach **Queimadas**, take any of the three morning Horários do Funchal number 56 buses to Santana, then a taxi. If you have made an early start you can walk the 4km from Santana, but it's mostly uphill and tiring in hot conditions.

Some 990m above sea level, **Queimadas Forest Park** is a delightful spot, with half-timbered forestry rest houses surrounding a duck pond amid a sea of verdant moss and ferns. Two popular

walking routes depart from here. One to Caldeirão Verde, the other to Pico das Pedras.

From Queimadas a red clay path riddled with tree roots runs along the levada. The first major obstacle the water course has to tackle are **two ravines** formed by the Ribeira dos Cedros and the Ribeira da Fonte do Louro. Not long after these are behind you comes the first short tunnel.

Three more **tunnels** follow in quick succession, so now is the time to get the torch out. The longest is the second one, which also includes a bend, so you can't see the end at the beginning. Watch your footwork as the floors are uneven and often wet – shine the torch about 5m in front of you and keep your head down.

Bird life is the other nature-spotter's highlight along this route. As on other levada walks, chaffinches have learnt which side their *bolo do caco* is buttered and will tamely eat from your outstretched palm. Others to look out for are the long-toed pigeon, the firecrest, the grey wagtail and the buzzard.

A short distance from the last tunnel, the **Caldeirão Verde** appears to the left (also pictured left). The 'Green Cauldron' is one of the prettiest spots on the island of Madeira: a waterfall gushing into a lake from a height of about 100m and encircled by a tall amphitheatre of plant life. It's a magic experience if you find yourself here alone.

Rabaçal–Levada do Risco & Levada das 25 Fontes

◦ **Start & Finish** Rabaçal

◦ **Length** 16km, 4 hours

On the southern edge of the Paúl da Serra, Rabaçal is a watery wonderland of springs and waterfalls, and the point where three levadas converge. This walk takes in two of them, and is one of the few levada trails on which you might meet day-tripping Funchalese.

There's simply no way to reach Rabaçal by public transport as no bus serves the ER110 road across the Paúl da Serra. Organising a ride from Calheta works out cheapest, otherwise you'll have to hire a car. The road to Rabaçal from the ER110 is closed to traffic, so you have to park and walk down.

Trails PR6 (Levada das 25 Fontes) and PR6.1 (Levada do Risco) both start at **Rabaçal** (1064m), the combined hiking distance of around 16km making a great day out. Starting at the Rabaçal houses, take the highest levada – the Levada do Risco. After

Hiking the Levada do Risco

about 30 minutes you should pass a fork in the path, the other route leading to 25 Fontes.

After just 10 minutes comes the wonderful **Risco Waterfall**, which plunges 100m into a lagoon. It's a romantic spot, especially if you can time a visit to avoid the tour groups. It will probably also be time for lunch, and there's no better picnic spot on the island.

Head back the way you came for 10 minutes until you reach the fork again. This time take the Levada das 25 Fontes. After 20 minutes you cross the riverbed of the **Ribeira Grande**, after which the channel narrows down considerably with drops on your left. Take care on this section.

In around 30 minutes you should reach the **25 Fontes**, another pool fed by numerous (though possibly not 25) waterfalls. Legend has it that anyone who submerges themselves in the lagoon will never resurface. Water from here eventually finds its way to the hydroelectric power station in Calheta. From here retrace your steps back to Rabaçal.

Explore ✦

Mountains of the Interior

Madeira's mountains rise from sea level to over 1800m in just 12km, meaning the interior is where the island's famous 'vertical reality' takes over. The sharp basalt peaks, plunging valleys and bottomless gorges are an adventure playground in the truest sense of the words. This is also where you'll find the best of Madeira's levada hikes and long-distance trails.

The Short List

○ **Curral das Freiras (p128)** Gazing in awe at the location of this village deep in a massive cauldron of rock.

○ **Rabaçal (p135)** Hiking the levadas of this verdantly lush mountainside.

○ **Pico do Arieiro (p135)** Getting up early to catch the sunrise from this easily-reachable peak.

○ **Ribeiro Frio (p136)** Cooling off at the beginning or end of a levada walk in 'Cold River'.

Getting There & Around

🚌 SAM, Rodoeste and Horários do Funchal all operate services into the mountains.

Interior Map on p134

Curral das Freiras (p128) JUERGEN SACK/GETTY IMAGES ©

Top Experience 📷
Curral das Freiras

The village of Curral das Freiras (Nun's Valley), set at the bottom of a huge cauldron of rock, is one of the most popular day trips from Funchal, and is home to that typical Madeiran combination of awe-inspiring mountain scenery, an easy-going walk, local specialities and welcoming locals. It's just a short (but almost vertical) bus ride from the bustle of Funchal's seafront.

◉ **MAP P134, D3**

www.jf-curraldasfreiras.pt

Hike from Eira do Serrado

A scenic way to approach Curral das Freiras is to take the bus to the lookout point at Eira do Serrado, 1094m above sea level, and hike down from there. Enjoy the truly astounding views down to the valley floor around 700m below before taking the downhill path from behind the hotel and souvenir stalls; a popular hike, the 4.5km route is downhill until the very last section along the road, mostly on rounded steps. On the way there, high outcrops of volcanic rock make excellent picnic halts, and interesting flora such as eucalyptus trees and camphor plants scent the air.

Chestnuts & Ginja

The village has several spots to sample some local specialities. Chestnuts are harvested here between October and January, but are available all year round as an ingredient in soup, bread, biscuits, cakes, liqueurs and sweets. The village even holds a Festa da Castanha (chestnut festival) in early November and 'exports' its products to the tourist hotspots of Funchal. Curral das Freiras is also known for its *ginja* – a cherry liqueur drunk across the island from shot glasses made of dark chocolate.

Village & Surroundings

Also worth a visit is the pretty Igreja de Nossa Senhora do Livramento, interesting for its cliff-edge position just off the main road. Around Curral das Freiras are remote-feeling settlements where locals grow vegetables in ever-steepening gradients the further up the valley you progress. A demanding hike heads straight up the side of a mountain from north of the village, linking in with the Encumeada–Boca do Corrida trail.

★ Top Tips

o It's a good idea to tackle the hike from Eira do Serrado downhill, though some do make the climb from Curral das Freiras.

o The path between Eira do Serrado and Curral das Freiras is safe, but care should be taken after heavy rain.

o Morning buses stop in Eira do Serrado, but later services miss it out.

o Last buses from Curral das Freiras leave late in the evening, so there's little chance of getting stranded.

✕ Take a Break

Vale das Freiras (p137) has a menu of traditional chestnut-based dishes.

Sabores do Curral (p137) has a slightly more gourmet feel and more international dishes.

Walking Tour 🥾

Pico do Arieiro to Pico Ruivo

Arguably the best walk on Madeira, this occasionally challenging mountain hike links the island's three highest peaks. The views are astounding, but come prepared – sturdy footwear, warm clothes, a torch, water and food are essentials. The walk can be done independently, but with rockfalls an issue, a guide is recommended.

Walk Facts

Start Pico do Arieiro
Finish Pico Ruivo
Length 5km, 4 hours

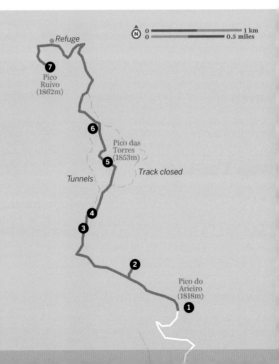

❶ Pico do Arieiro

Early mornings are busy at the top of Pico do Arieiro, Madeira's third-highest mountain (1818m). Some people are having breakfast in the cafe with the best view from any Madeiran eatery, others are making adjustments to kit or just taking snaps of the surrounding mountainscape. But PR1, the trail to Pico Ruivo, awaits.

❷ Ninho da Manta

Around 20 minutes into the hike, the first stop for most is Ninho da Manta, or Buzzard's Nest, a *miradouro* (viewpoint) with astounding views down to the Penha D'Aguía (the Eagle's Rock), a huge coastal mountain that locals claim looks like the head of an eagle.

❸ Túnel do Pico do Gato

After around 45 minutes that torch you brought comes in handy as you enter the almost complete darkness of the first tunnel on the route, túnel do Pico do Gato. Pico do Gato – Cat's Peak – refers to the mountain you see as you emerge back into the sun/fog.

❹ Fork in the Road

One hour in, the path splits. To the left is the easier route through several tunnels. To the right is a longer, harder path. We are going right.

❺ Pico das Torres

After a long climb, a split in the rock at around the one-hour-40-minute mark announces you have arrived at Pico das Torres (1853m), Madeira's second-highest mountain. Pico Ruivo is seemingly just across the way, but still two hours distant.

❻ Take the Tunnel

At around the 2½-hour mark, there's another split in the path, but this time the decision about which way to go has been taken for you. A barrier has been erected to prevent hikers accessing the old dangerous path. Take the tunnel to access the new trail.

❼ Pico Ruivo

By the three-hours-40-minute mark you should reach the mountain refuge just below Pico Ruivo (1862m). Many call it a day here, but the top is only half a kilometre away and it's worth it for the stupendous views.

Walking Tour 🚶

Boca da Corrida to Encumeada

The dramatic path, known as the Caminha Real da Encumeada, was one of the main horse and foot routes across the island before roads were built. The clearly marked and well-maintained trail skirts the foot of some of Madeira's highest peaks, taking you well above the tree line. This route should not be tackled in high winds or when heavy rain is forecast.

Walk Facts

Start Boca da Corrida

Finish Estalgem Encumeada

Length 13.3km, 4 hours

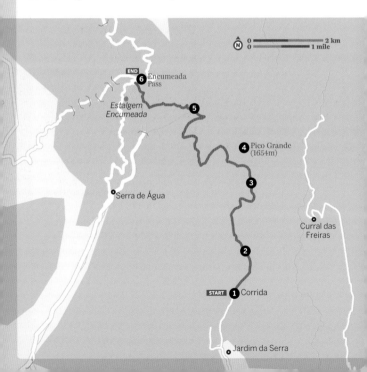

❶ Corrida

Rodoeste bus 96 leaves Funchal twice in the morning for Corrida. Just the ride, a seemingly almost vertical climb from Câmara de Lobos, is an invigorating start to the day. Buses deposit hikers at a lonely terminus from where it's a stiff climb up an asphalt road to the start of the hike.

❷ Boca da Corrida

It takes a good half an hour to reach Boca da Corrida, the start of the walk. Here you'll find a tiny chapel and views across the mammoth valley at the top of which is the village of Curral das Freiras.

❸ Boca de Cerro

By the time you reach the Boca de Cerro (1¼ hours), it's probably time for lunch and this is a good spot to de-bag supplies. An alternative walk from here is to take the badly signposted trail down to Curral das Freiras, though this is an extremely steep, exposed route.

❹ Escarpment of Pico Grande

After Boca de Cerro the path narrows, but is still very easy to pick out. At the 90-minute mark you begin to edge your way around the base of the escarpment of Pico Grande, one of the island's highest mountains.

❺ Ribeira do Poço Valley

From Pico Grande the path begins its descent towards Encumeada. After around 2½ hours you enter the valley of the Ribeira do Poço, a lush and verdant stretch that contrasts markedly with the bare rock the path has crossed for most of the way.

❻ Encumeada

The path weaves its way down to the valley until it becomes a track. This leads to the main road, which crosses the Encumeada Pass. From here you can walk down to the Estalgem Encumeada for a coffee and catch the bus back to Funchal (Rodoeste buses 6 and 139). Check the timetables before you leave Funchal.

Mountains of the Interior

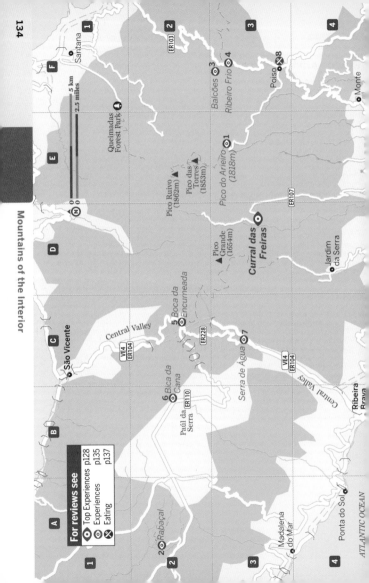

For reviews see

◉ Top Experiences p128
◎ Experiences p135
✕ Eating p137

Santana

São Vicente

Queimadas
Forest Park

Central Valley

0   5 km
0   2.5 miles

Pico Ruivo
(1862m) ▲

Pico das
Torres
(1853m) ▲

Pico do Arieiro
(1818m) ◉1

ER103

Balcões ◉3

Ribeiro Frio ◉4

Poiso ◉✕8

Monte

Pico
Grande
(1654m) ▲

Curral das
Freiras ◉

Jardim
da Serra

ER107

Boca da
Encumeada 5◉

ER228

Serra de Água ◉7

VE4
ER104

Central Valley

Ribeira
Brava

Bica da
Cana 6◉

Paúl da
Serra ER110

VE4
ER104

Rabaçal 2◉

Madalena
do Mar

Ponta do Sol

ATLANTIC OCEAN

Experiences

Pico do Arieiro · MOUNTAIN

1 MAP P134, E3

You can drive to the top of Pico do Arieiro, Madeira's third highest mountain. At the top you'll find a cafe, a Portuguese Air Force radar station and stupendous views. Try to get up here for the sunrise, though you'll not enjoy the spectacle alone. To get here, take the northwest turn-off from the ER103 at Poiso. (off ER103)

Rabaçal · WATERFALL

2 MAP P134, A2

The waterfalls, springs and hiking trails at Rabaçal are an easy-going highlight of Madeira's outdoor world. You can spend all day cooling off in the cascades and pools, inspecting the ferns and counting the 25 Fontes (25 waterfalls). Trips leave daily from Funchal – there's no public transport. A new *abrigo* (mountain guesthouse) means you can now stay the night here, though it only has a handful of beds. The waterfalls are 60km northwest of Funchal, off the ER105. (off ER105; ⏱24hr)

Balcões · VIEWPOINT

3 MAP P134, F3

A 1.5km easy and well-signposted climb out of the village of Ribeiro Frio brings you to one of the most spectacular viewing points on the whole of Madeira, the aptly named Balcões – the Balconies. From here you get a bird's eye view of the island's highest peaks, the

Balcões

huge cauldron of rock below them and even out across the Atlantic to the island of Porto Santo. A snack bar hangs off the cliff edge half way along the path. (Ribeiro Frio)

Ribeiro Frio VILLAGE

4 ⊙ MAP P134, F3

'Cold River' village, deep in the mountains but under the tree line, is the chilly jumping off point for some levada walks and has a couple of cosy restaurants serving local trout and heated with log fires. Makes for an interesting stop between Funchal and Santana. (ER103)

Boca da Encumeada LANDMARK

5 ⊙ MAP P134, C2

The Encumeada Pass sits between the two deep-cleft valleys that almost slice Madeira in two. From this dramatic point 1083m up, you can see both the north and south coastlines. It's also the starting point for several hikes and long-distance

Paúl da Serra

Overlooked by most tourists, the lonely Paúl da Serra is a high flat plateau of treeless moorland inhabited by Madeira's only cows. It was once suggested that Madeira's airport be moved up here – until someone counted how many days a year these uplands are smothered in fog.

trails. A tunnel under Encumeada means 99% of traffic now bypasses the pass. (ER228, Encumeada)

Bica da Cana VIEWPOINT

6 ⊙ MAP P134, B2

High above the central valley at the eastern end of the Paúl da Serra plateau is a place called Bica da Cana. Apart from serving as a picnic spot for cross-island travellers, it also offers widescreen views of Madeira's highest peaks across the valley. It's well known for its wind farm, a controversial addition to this highly visible location. (ER110)

Serra de Água VILLAGE

7 ⊙ MAP P134, C3

Jammed into the central valley that cleaves Madeira asunder, this picturesque village of 1000 souls is slightly off the beaten track. It's surrounded by high mountains and terraces on which locals grow produce. (ER104)

Ribeiro Frio Trout Farm FARM

Apart from being the launch pad for some great mountain walks, Ribeiro Frio's other attraction (see 4 ⊙ Map p134, F3) is what must be the world's most visited trout farm. Hundreds of trout chase each other around huge tanks fed with icy cold levada water, the whole place a fishy, multilevel symphony of moving water. Don't feed the fish, whatever you do – it's strictly forbidden. (ER103, Ribeiro Frio; admission free; 24hr)

Eating

Restaurante Ribeiro Frio
MADEIRAN $$

This cosy pre- or post-levada-hike refuge (see 4 ◉ Map p134, F3) is good for a full-blown, calorie-replacing meal, or coffee and cakes while you wait for the bus back to Funchal. With the trout farm almost opposite, it's no surprise that the rare freshwater fish dominates the menu. The wood-rich interior is warmed by cast-iron stoves, a welcome sight after a day on a damp levada. (Ribeiro Frio; mains €7-15; ◷9am-7pm)

Casa de Abrigo do Poiso
PORTUGUESE, MADEIRAN $$

8 ✖ MAP P134, F3

At the turn off on the ER103 for Pico do Arieiro, this rustic mountain refuge plates up Portuguese and Madeiran favourites in a welcoming, slightly old-fashioned dining room. It's just the place to reheat after a hike in the hills with a few shots of *poncha* (local sugar-cane spirit drink) and a bowl of hearty and warming Madeiran tomato soup. (www.casaabrigopoiso. ondebiz.com; ER103, Poiso; mains €8-16; ◷8.30pm-midnight Mon, 8.30am-midnight Tue-Thu & Sun, 8.30pm-2am Fri & Sat)

Sabores do Curral
MADEIRAN $$

The 'Flavours of Curral' is the pinnacle of the dining scene in this tourist hotspot (see ◉ Map p134, D3). After admiring one of the most gob-smacking, cliff-edge views you'll ever experience from any restaurant, choose from the simple but well-executed menu of traditional Madeiran meat and fish dishes, with a snifter of local *ginja* (cherry liqueur) to start. (☏291 712 257; Caminho da Igreja 1, Curral das Freiras; mains €8-15; ◷9am-6pm Tue-Sun)

Vale das Freiras
MADEIRAN $$

Curral das Freiras (see ◉ Map p134, D3) is known for its chestnuts and this restaurant-cafe specialises in all sorts of dishes made from them. Chestnut soup, liqueurs, cakes, bread or just plain roasted chestnuts are the highlights of the menu, though there are other Madeiran staples, too. There's a complimentary chestnut liqueur for everyone and an adjoining shop selling more... yes you guessed it, chestnuts. (Caminho de Padaria 2, Curral das Freiras; mains €5-15; ◷8am-10pm)

Top Experience 📷
Porto Santo

You may hear or read the word 'archipelago' in relation to Madeira – that's because the main island is not alone. The Desertas and Selvagens islands are uninhabited, but 40km to the northeast, Madeira's sister island, Porto Santo, has a population of around 5500. Measuring just 14km by 8km, Porto Santo is a very different place to Madeira. It's arid, low-slung and boasts one of Europe's finest golden-sand beaches – the main reason to make the journey here.

✈ Binter Canarias operate two flights a day from Madeira Airport.

⚓ Porto Santo Line runs a daily ferry to/from Funchal.

Staying the Night

Porto Santo is touted as a day cruise from Funchal, the small ferry leaving in the morning and returning in the evening. This suits visitors with little time on their hands, but to really savour this remote outpost of the Portuguese world, consider an overnight stay. This allows you to enjoy a day on the beach and another exploring the island by bicycle or scooter. There are plenty of hotels around Vila Baleira, some offering great deals outside the summer months. The town also boasts the archipelago's biggest campsite (there are only two!), but you'll need to bring a tent.

Vila Baleira

The only settlement of any size is sleepy Vila Baleira, where you'll find the **turismo** (☎291 985 244; Avenida Dr Manuel Gregório Pestana Junior, Vila Baleira; ⏱9am-12.30pm & 2-5.30pm Mon-Fri, 10am-12.30pm Sat) and all the island's services. It's one of the archipelago's oldest towns, founded in 1419 by the first governor, Bartolomeu Perestrelo. Pretty, whitewashed Largo do Pelhourinho has a beautiful old church and lots of cafe tables.

The Beach

Extending about 7.5km from the ferry port to the island's southernmost point, Ponta da Calheta, Porto Santo's beach (pictured left) is nothing short of spectacular; it is regularly voted one of the top 10 stretches of sand in Europe (though it's not actually in Europe). The large grains are tiny fragments of coral, the remains of reefs dating back 20 million years. Gently shelving into the cooling Atlantic and backed by Porto Santo's long-since-extinct volcano cones, this is a place you'll want to linger until the ferry departs. In summer the beach attracts Portuguese families escaping the heat of the mainland; in winter you can have it to yourself.

★ **Top Tips**

○ The ferry to Porto Santo is often cancelled due to bad weather – but no refunds are offered, but you can rebook.

○ The island is best visited in the summer months when things are livelier.

○ Car and scooter hire is available (on the seafront in Vila Baleira), so there's no need to bring your own hire car.

✕ **Take a Break**

Pé na Água (Sítio das Pedras Pretas; mains €10-20; ⏱11am-11pm) is a beach restaurant and bar to the west of Vila Baleira

Baiana (Largo do Pelhourinho; mains €5-10; ⏱9am-1am), on the square in Vila Baleira, is a convenient, popular and informal restaurant.

Columbus & Porto Santo

Local myth paints a romantic picture – a 27-year-old Columbus, strolling Porto Santo's jaw-droppingly beautiful beach, picking up exotic seeds washed up by the Atlantic, looking to the horizon and wondering what might lie beyond...

But how did the man who went on to 'discover' the Americas come to be on this micro-island in the Atlantic? Commissioned to buy sugar on Madeira by a Lisbon merchant house, Columbus arrived in Funchal in 1478. He probably knew Porto Santo's governor, Bartolomeu Perestrelo II, son of the island's first governor, from their early days in Genoa. Columbus married his daughter, Dona Felipa Moniz, that same year and moved to Madeira's lesser sibling. But in 1479 tragedy struck when Felipa and their newborn son died, leaving Columbus alone to wander and wonder. He left soon after and the rest, as they say in these parts, is *história*.

Columbus House

The island's only bona fide 'sight' is the **Casa Museu Colombo** (www.museucolombo-portosanto.com; Travessa da Sacristia 2/4, Vila Baleira; admission €2; ⏲10am-noon & 2-5.30pm Tue-Sat, 10am-1pm Sun Oct-Jun, to 7pm Tue-Sat Jul-Sep), just off Largo do Pelhourinho. It's claimed Christopher Columbus lived here. The museum contains exhibitions on the colonisation of the New World and Columbus' voyages, but as there's no real evidence Columbus actually lived in this particular house, the information on the explorer is a bit vague and based more on popular myth than historical fact.

Volcanic Peaks

Porto Santo is a much older island than Madeira (by around 13 million years) and the volcanoes that pushed through the Atlantic's surface have been worn down by rain and wind into odd-shaped peaks. The highest of these is **Pico do Facho** (516m), northeast of Vila Baleira, where fires were once lit to warn Madeira of impending pirate attacks. Directly north of the 'capital' is **Pico Castelo** (437m) and in the far southwest is **Pico de Ana Ferreira** (283m), both of which can be climbed for magnificent Macaronesian views.

Rest of the Island

If you hire a bike, scooter or car, the island can be seen in a couple of hours. Porto Santo's airport is an odd spectacle, extending almost the entire width of the island. **Porto Santo Golfe** (☎291 983 778; www.portosantogolfe.com; Sítio das Marinhas) is arguably the archipelago's best course. Designed by Seve Ballesteros, its 18 holes regularly make it into the world's top 100 golf courses. The Portela viewpoint provides views of the whole island and is a popular 2½-hour hike from Vila Baleira; ask at the tourist office for details.

ATLANTIC OCEAN

Pico de Facho (516m)

Pico Castelo (437m)

Airport

Vila Baleira

Beach

Ferry Port

Porto Santo Golfe

Pico de Ana Ferreira (283m)

Funchal

Ilhéu de Baixo

N

0   2 km
0   1 mile

Survival Guide

Ribeira Brava (p24) TATIANA POPOVA/SHUTTERSTOCK ©

Before You Go

Book Your Stay

○ The vast majority of Madeira's visitors stay in Funchal, most of them in the Hotel Zone to the city's west.

○ Funchal has everything from 1970s two-star hotels to five-star opulence.

○ The most stylish and quintessentially Madeiran accommodation is hotels created out of quintas, the island's old mansion houses.

○ Renting a flat or a villa through popular booking websites has become popular in recent years, though it's not as widespread as in other destinations.

Useful Websites

○ **Lonely Planet** (www. lonelyplanet.com) Author recommendations, reviews and online booking.

○ **Madeira Apartments** (www.madeiraapartments.com) Villas, cottages and apartments in a variety of locations.

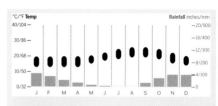

°C/°F Temp — Rainfall inches/mm

When to Go

○ **Feb** Carnival time when the island is at its busiest and brightest.

○ **Jul-Aug** Hottest weather, least rain and all bathing areas open.

○ **Dec** Funchal puts on an amazing show for the end of the year.

○ **Madeira Web** (www. madeira-web.com) All of Madeira's best hotels on one site.

Best Budget

○ **29 Madeira Hostel** (www.29madeirahostel. com) Funchal's newest hostel in a beautifully restored 1930s city-centre town house.

○ **Santa Maria Hostel** (www.santamariafunchal.com) Large hostel in a former Zona Velha school with a top-notch restaurant and bar.

○ **Parque de Campismo Porto Moniz** (www.portomoniz.pt) The only campsite on Madeira, located in Ribeira da Janela near Porto Moniz.

Best Midrange

○ **Estalgem Ponta do Sol** (www.pontadosol. com) Stylish, minimalist hotel on the cliff above Ponta do Sol seafront.

○ **Quinta Splendida** (www.quintasplendida. com) Well-appointed hotel in Caniço with rooms spread throughout a set of stunningly exotic Madeiran gardens.

○ **Dom Pedro Madeira** (www.dompedrobaia hotel.com) Machico's top hotel with superb views of the bay, comfortable rooms and a central location.

○ **Hotel Monte Carlo** (www.hotelmontecarlo-madeira.pt) Old-fashioned and authentic hotel located high above the city centre.

Best Top End

○ **Reid's Palace** (www.belmond.com) Still traditionally Madeira's most illustrious hotel with a star-studded guest list.

○ **The Vine** (www.hotelthevine.com) One of Europe's finest design hotels in downtown Funchal.

○ **Savoy Calheta Beach** (www.savoycalhetabeach.com) Right on the beach in Calheta, with contemporary rooms and a good restaurant.

○ **Cliff Bay** (www.portobay.com) A luxurious, award-winning hotel in Funchal's Hotel Zone.

Arriving in Madeira

Madeira Airport

○ Madeira Airport is 19km from central Funchal. The journey takes around 25 minutes by car and 40 minutes by bus.

○ **SAM** (☎291 201 151; www.sam.pt) runs Aero-bus shuttles (single/return €5/8, 4am to 8pm) at least hourly between the airport and Praia

Formosa via Funchal city centre and the Hotel Zone.

○ **Madeira Airport Transfers** (☎913 756 539; www.madeira-airport-transfers.com; one-way trip €23) offers rides to and from Madeira airport, bookable online.

Cruise Terminal

○ Funchal is reachable on foot in around 15 minutes.

○ From the centre take bus 01, 02 or 04 to the Hotel Zone.

Porto Santo Airport

○ The only way to get from the airport in Porto Santo is by taxi. These wait at the terminal when flights are due.

Getting Around

Bus

○ If you aren't hiring a car then you'll need to take a bus to get anywhere on the island.

○ The three main companies operating routes are **SAM** (☎291 201 151; www.sam.pt; east of Funchal and airport shuttle), **Rodoeste** (www.rodoeste.com.pt; west of Funchal) and **Horários do Funchal** (☎291 705 555; www.horariosdofunchal.pt; Anadia Shopping Centre, Rua Visconde de Anadia; ⏱main ticket & information office 8.30am-7pm Mon-Fri), who provide Funchal

---

Useful Bus Services

○ **Horários do Funchal** (urban routes) 01, 02, 04 city centre–Hotel Zone; 48 Hotel Zone–Monte; 20/21 city centre–Monte; 22 city centre–Babosas.

○ **Horários do Funchal** (interurban routes) – 56/103 Santana via Ribeiro Frio; 81 Curral das Freiras; 113 Camacha.

○ **Rodoeste** 80 Porto Moniz; 139 Porto Moniz via São Vicente and Encumeada; 6 Encumeada; 7 Ribeira Brava.

○ **SAM** 23 Machico; 113 Baía D'Abra via Machico and Caniçal.

city buses plus some mountain services).

o All have online time-tables and run a reliable service.

o There are consider-ably fewer buses at weekends.

o The vast majority of services originate and terminate in Funchal, but there are some obscure, mid-afternoon buses between other towns.

Car & Motorcycle

o Many visitors hire a car while on Madeira. Having your own set of wheels makes things a lot easier and you will see more.

o The Via Rápida motor-way links Machico with Ribeira Brava via the airport and Funchal, and has cut journey times immensely.

o Away from the motorway, roads are frequently steep, narrow and twisting so you'll need to be confident behind the wheel.

o An odd phenomenon on the island are the natural 'car washes', wa-terfalls that sluice down onto roads after rain. Debris on the road after rock falls and intense wind/rain are other things to watch out for.

o There are several hire companies operating in Madeira, including Auto Jardim (www.carhire madeira.net) and Guerin (www.guerin.pt). **Rodavante** (☑291 524

718; www.rodavante.com) is a local company with branches at the airport and in the Hotel Zone.

Taxi

o Some visitors use taxis to tour the island.

o Madeiran taxis are always yellow with a blue stripe along the side. The most common vehicles are Mercedes saloons and Mercedes minivans.

o Fares are €2.50 pick-up charge (€3 at night and weekends) plus €0.66 (€0.79) per kilometre. You might also pay for baggage.

o In Funchal fares are metered.

o Outside Funchal you can often haggle the unmetered price down a bit at quiet times.

o Many taxi owners/ companies also run excursions and island tours. Expect to pay around €25 to €35 per person for a full day.

o Hotel receptions can always summon a trust-worthy taxi for you.

o Some taxis tout for business at bus stops. Don't encourage this by accepting a ride.

Money-saving Tips

o Calculate how many journeys you are likely to make on Funchal's buses and charge up your Girocard accordingly.

o Prebook your airport transfer and pay for it withPayPal.

o Use buses rather than taxis to access the levadas.

o Organise hikes yourself rather than going with a tour group.

o Never accept the first price drivers suggest when taking a taxi outside Funchal.

o Eat in supermarket Pingo Doce's excellent, self-service, pay-by-weight restaurants.

Boat

o The archipelago's ferry service is **Porto Santo Line** (📞291 210 300; www. portosantoline.pt; return €47.50-58.10), which runs to Porto Santo once daily.

o Other nonscheduled tour services operate to the Desertas Islands and out to sea for fishing and wildlife-spotting trips.

Cable Car

o Madeira has several useful cable cars, the most frequented being the routes running from Zona Velha to Monte and from Monte to the Botanical Gardens.

Essential Information

Accessible Travel

o Modern hotels in the Hotel Zone must have disabled facilities by law.

o Buses between the Hotel Zone and the city centre have disabled access.

o Outside Funchal things are not particularly wheelchair-friendly.

o The cable car to Monte has disabled access.

o Some 2km of the Pico das Pedras to Queimadas trail has been made wheelchair accessible.

Electricity

**Type F
230V/50Hz**

Money

o Madeira uses the euro (€) as its currency.

o ATMs are widespread - every village has at least one.

o Payment by card is common, though there are situations (buses, small cafes, markets) where you will need cash.

o Tipping is rarely expected.

Opening Hours

Smaller shops close on Sundays but malls and supermarkets are open every day. Standard opening hours:

Shops 9am to 7pm

Museums 10am to 12.30pm, 2pm to 6pm

Post Offices 8.30am to 8pm Monday to Friday, 9am to 1pm Saturday

Restaurants noon to 3pm, 6pm to 11pm

Public Holidays

New Year's Day 1 January

Carnaval (Jan/Feb) 40 days before Easter Monday

Easter March/April

Liberation Day 25 April

Labour Day 1 May

National Day 10 June

Madeira Day 1 July

Assumption 15 August

Funchal City Day 21 August

Republic Day 5 October

All Saints Day 1 November

Restoration of Independence 1 December

Dos & Don'ts

○ Smart-casual attire may be expected in some upmarket restaurants and places of entertainment.

○ Always allow locals with children to board buses first. If you are travelling with children, locals (though possibly not tourists) will do the same.

○ Give up your seat on buses to the elderly and to children.

○ Don't encourage taxis touting at bus stops by accepting rides.

○ Do learn a few phrases of Portuguese – Madeirans are very polite and appreciate the odd *bom dia* (hello) and *obrigado* (thank you) from foreigners.

Immaculate Conception 8 December

Christmas Day 25 December

1st Octave 26 December

Safe Travel

○ Every year a couple of hikers have accidents on the levadas – these are sometimes fatal. Be extra careful on narrow exposed sections and never try to walk after dark.

○ There has been a noticeable increase in touting, especially along Funchal seafront. While they're polite, they can be irritating.

○ Only confident drivers should hire cars on Madeira. Never take shortcuts when behind the wheel.

○ Rock falls are an issue – stay well away from any areas signposted as dangerous.

○ Don't underestimate the weather at altitude. While sunbathers frolic in the Hotel Zone, there can be snow at Pico do Arieiro.

Toilets

○ Toilets are widespread across the island and always free.

○ Gentlemen's toilets are often marked with the letter 'H' (homens), the Ladies with an 'S' (senhoras).

Tourist Information

○ The main **turismo** (☎291 211 902; www.visitmadeira.pt; Avenida Arriaga 16; ⏰9am-8pm Mon-Fri, 9am-3.30pm Sat & Sun) can field most questions though staff can be a bit flummoxed and visitor-weary.

○ There are other branches at the airport, at the Centro Comercial Monumental, at the cruise terminal and in Curral das Freiras, Santana, Porto Moniz, Vila Baleira and Ribeira Brava.

○ Funchal now has its own **municipal tourist office** (☎291 223 949; www.visitfunchal.pt; Praça do Povo, Avenida do Mar; ⏰8.30am-7.30pm Mon-Fri, to 1.30pm Sat).

Visas

○ As an autonomous region of Portugal, Madeira is part of the Schengen zone.

○ EU nationals can stay indefinitely.

○ All other nationals should check with their Portuguese embassy.

Language

Most sounds in Portuguese are also found in English. The exceptions are the nasal vowels (represented in our pronunciation guides by 'ng' after the vowel), pronounced as if you're trying to make the sound through your nose; and the strongly rolled *r* (represented by '*rr*' in our pronunciation guides). Also note that the symbol '*zh*' sounds like the 's' in 'pleasure'. Keeping these few points in mind and reading the pronunciation guides as if they were English, you'll be understood just fine. The stressed syllables are indicated with italics.

To enhance your trip with a phrasebook, visit lonelyplanet.com.

Basics

Hello.
Olá. o·laa

Goodbye.
Adeus. a·de·oosh

How are you?
Como está? ko·moo shtaa

Fine, and you?
Bem, e você? beng e vo·se

Please.
Por favor. poor fa·vor

Thank you.
Obrigado. (m) o·bree·gaa·doo
Obrigada. (f) o·bree·gaa·da

Excuse me.
Faz favor. faash fa·vor

Sorry.
Desculpe. desh·kool·pe

Yes./No.
Sim./Não. seeng/nowng

I don't understand.
Não entendo. nowng eng·teng·doo

Do you speak English?
Fala inglês? faa·la eeng·glesh

Eating & Drinking

..., please. *..., por favor.* ... poor fa·vor

A coffee *Um café* oong ka·fe

**A table
for two** *Uma mesa* oo·ma me·za
para duas pa·ra doo·ash
pessoas pe·so·ash

Two beers *Dois* doysh
cervejas ser·ve·zhash

I'm a vegetarian.
Eu sou e·oo soh
vegetariano/ ve·zhe·a·ree·a·noo/
vegetariana. (m/f) ve·zhe·a·ree·a·na

Cheers!
Saúde! sa·oo·de

That was delicious!
Isto estava eesh·too shtaa·va
delicioso. de·lee·see·o·zoo

The bill, please.
A conta, por favor. a kong·ta poor
fa·vor

Shopping

I'd like to buy ...
Queria ke·ree·a
comprar ... kong·praar ...

I'm just looking.
Estou só a ver. shtoh so a ver

How much is it?
Quanto custa? kwang·too
koosh·ta

It's too expensive.
Está muito shtaa mweeng·too
caro. kaa·roo

Can you lower the price?
Pode baixar po·de bai·shaar
o preço? oo pre·soo

Emergencies

Help!
Socorro! soo·ko·rroo

Call a doctor!
Chame um shaa·me oong
médico! me·dee·koo

Call the police!
Chame a shaa·me a
polícia! poo·lee·sya

I'm sick.
Estou doente. shtoh doo·eng·te

I'm lost.
Estou perdido. (m) shtoh per·dee·doo
Estou perdida. (f) shtoh per·dee·da

Where's the toilet?
Onde é a casa de ong·de e a kaa·za de
banho? ba·nyoo

Time & Numbers

What time is it?
Que horas são? kee o·rash sowng

It's (10) o'clock.
São (dez) horas. sowng (desh)
o·rash

Half past (10).
(Dez) e meia. (desh) e may·a

morning	manhã	ma·nyang
afternoon	tarde	taar·de
evening	noite	noy·te
yesterday	ontem	ong·teng

today	hoje	o·zhe
tomorrow	amanhã	aa·ma·nyang

1	um	oong
2	dois	doysh
3	três	tresh
4	quatro	kwaa·troo
5	cinco	seeng·koo
6	seis	saysh
7	sete	se·te
8	oito	oy·too
9	nove	no·ve
10	dez	desh

Transport & Directions

Where's ...?
Onde é ...? ong·de e ...

What's the address?
Qual é o kwaal e oo
endereço? eng·de·re·soo

Can you show me (on the map)?
Pode-me po·de·me
mostrar moosh·traar
(no mapa)? (noo maa·pa)

When's the next bus?
Quando é que sai kwang·doo e ke sai
o próximo oo pro·see·moo
autocarro? ow·to·kaa·rroo

I want to go to ...
Queria ir a ... ke·ree·a eer a ...

Does it stop at ...?
Pára em ...? paa·ra eng ...

Please stop here.
Por favor pare poor fa·vor paa·re
aqui. a·kee

Behind the Scenes

Send Us Your Feedback

We love to hear from travellers – your comments help make our books better. We read every word, and we guarantee that your feedback goes straight to the authors. Visit **lonelyplanet.com/contact** to submit your updates and suggestions.

Note: We may edit, reproduce and incorporate your comments in Lonely Planet products such as guidebooks, websites and digital products, so let us know if you don't want your comments reproduced or your name acknowledged. For a copy of our privacy policy visit lonelyplanet.com/privacy.

Our Readers

Many thanks to the travellers who used the last edition and wrote to us with helpful hints, useful advice and interesting anecdotes: Chris Hall, David Holborow, Ian Coldicott, Ian Martin, Julie Robinson, Lasse Kehler, Patrick Anthony, Sarah Beck, Venetia Caine.

Marc's Thanks

A big *obrigado* to Sandra Gouveia of the Madeira Promotion Bureau, João Caldeira in Funchal, all the staff at tourist offices around Madeira, and my wife for holding the fort at home while I was away.

Acknowledgements

Cover photograph: Pico do Arieiro, Mauricio Abreu / AWL ©

Photographs p32-3 (clockwise from top left): Juergen Sack/Getty Images©, Dziewul/Shutterstock©, Pawel Kazmierczak/Shutterstock©

This Book

This second edition of Lonely Planet's *Pocket Madeira* guidebook was researched and written by Marc Di Duca, who also researched and wrote the previous edition. This guidebook was produced by the following:

Destination Editor Tom Stainer

Senior Product Editor Jessica Ryan

Regional Senior Cartographer Anthony Phelan

Product Editor Joel Cotterell

Book Designer Fergal Condon

Assisting Editors Lorna Parkes, Gabrielle Stefanos

Cover Researcher Naomi Parker

Thanks to Sandra Henriques Gajjar, Paul Harding, Kate James, Catherine Naghten, Angela Tinson

Index

See also separate subindexes for:

⊗ **Eating p154**
◉ **Drinking p155**
◈ **Entertainment p155**
⊡ **Shopping p155**

Sights 000
Map Pages 000

Drinking

Entertainment

Shopping